# 30 DEVOTIONALS

# GOD'S PLAN *for* YOUR LIFE
# OVERCOMING TOUGH TIMES

## BIBLICAL PRINCIPLES TO GUIDE YOU IN YOUR JOURNEY THROUGH TOUGH TIMES

# FAMILY
## Christian Stores®

Scripture quotations are taken from:

The Holy Bible, King James Version (KJV)

The Holy Bible, New International Version (NIV) Copyright © 1973, 1978, 1984, by International Bible Society. Used by permission of Zondervan Publishing House. All rights reserved.

The Holy Bible, New King James Version (NKJV) Copyright © 1982 by Thomas Nelson, Inc. Used by permission.

Holy Bible, New Living Translation, (NLT) copyright © 1996. Used by permission of Tyndale House Publishers, Inc., Wheaton, Illinois 60189. All rights reserved.

The Message (MSG)- This edition issued by contractual arrangement with NavPress, a division of The Navigators, U.S.A. Originally published by NavPress in English as THE MESSAGE: The Bible in Contemporary Language copyright 2002-2003 by Eugene Peterson. All rights reserved.

New Century Version®. (NCV) Copyright © 1987, 1988, 1991 by Word Publishing, a division of Thomas Nelson, Inc. All rights reserved. Used by permission.

The New American Standard Bible®, (NASB) Copyright © 1960, 1962, 1963, 1968, 1971, 1972, 1973, 1975, 1977, 1995 by The Lockman Foundation. Used by permission.

The Holman Christian Standard Bible™ (HCSB) Copyright © 1999, 2000, 2001 by Holman Bible Publishers. Used by permission.

Cover Design & Page Layout by Bart Dawson

ISBN 978-1-58334-014-1

Printed in the United States of America

# GOD'S PLAN *for* YOUR LIFE
# OVERCOMING TOUGH TIMES

BIBLICAL PRINCIPLES TO GUIDE YOU
IN YOUR JOURNEY THROUGH TOUGH TIMES

# TABLE OF CONTENTS

# INTRODUCTION

*"We know that all things work together
for the good of those who love God:
those who are called according to His purpose."*

Romans 8:28 HCSB

God's Word promises that all things work together for the good of those who love Him. Yet sometimes we encounter situations that seem so troubling that we simply cannot comprehend how these events might be a part of God's plan for our lives. We experience tough times: perhaps the loss of money or health; perhaps divorce, job loss, or a broken personal relationship. And we honestly wonder if recovery is possible. But with God, all things are possible.

The Christian faith, as communicated through the words of the Holy Bible, is a healing faith. It offers comfort in times of trouble, courage for our fears, hope instead of hopelessness. Through the healing words of God's promises, Christians understand that the Lord continues to manifest His plan in good times and bad.

If you are experiencing the pain of a recent setback, or if you are still mourning a loss from long ago, this book is intended to help. So, during the next 30 days, try this experiment: read one chapter a day and take the ideas in that chapter to heart. Then, apply those lessons to the everyday realities of your life. When you weave God's message into the fabric of your day, you'll quickly discover that God's Word has the power to change everything, including you.

Adversity is not meant to be feared, it is meant to be worked through. If this text assists you, even in a small way, as you move through and beyond your own tough times, it will have served its purpose. May God bless you and keep you, and may He place His hand upon your heart today and forever.

# Day 1

# GOD'S PLAN AND YOUR TOUGH TIMES

*"For I know the plans I have for you," declares the Lord,*
*"plans to prosper you and not to harm you, plans to give*
*you hope and a future. Then you will call upon me*
*and come and pray to me, and I will listen to you."*

Jeremiah 29:11-12 NIV

## THE FOCUS FOR TODAY

When terrible things happen, there are two choices,
and only two: We can trust God, or we can defy Him.
We believe that God is God, He's still got the whole
world in His hands and knows exactly what He's doing,
or we must believe that He is not God
and that we are at the awful mercy of mere chance.

Elisabeth Elliot

I t's an age-old riddle: Why does God allow us to endure tough times? After all, since we trust that God is all-powerful, and since we trust that His hand shapes our lives, why doesn't He simply rescue us—and our loved ones—from all hardship and pain?

God's Word teaches us again and again that He loves us and wants the best for us. And the Bible also teaches us that God is ever-present and always watchful. So why, we wonder, if God is really so concerned with every detail of our lives, does He permit us to endure emotions like grief, sadness, shame, or fear? And why does He allow tragic circumstances to invade the lives of good people? These questions perplex us, especially when times are tough.

On occasion, all of us face adversity, and throughout life, we all must endure life-changing personal losses that leave us breathless. When we pass through the dark valleys of life, we often ask, "Why me?" Sometimes, of course, the answer is obvious—sometimes we make mistakes, and we must pay for them. But on other occasions, when we have done nothing wrong, we wonder why God allows us to suffer.

Even when we cannot understand God's plans, we must trust them. And even when we are impatient for our situations to improve, we must trust God's timing. If we seek to live in accordance with His plan for our lives, we must continue to study His Word (in good times and bad), and we must be watchful for His signs, knowing that in time, He will lead us through the valleys, onward to the mountaintop.

So if you're enduring tough times, don't give up and don't give in. God still has glorious plans for you. So keep your eyes and ears open . . . as well as your heart.

## FINDING NEW MEANING

Perhaps tough times have turned your world upside down. Maybe it seems to you as if everything in your life has been rearranged. Or perhaps your relationships and your responsibilities have been permanently altered. If so, you may come face to face with the daunting task of finding a new purpose for your life. And God is willing to help.

God has an important plan for your life, and part of His plan may well be related to the tough times you're experiencing. After all, you've learned important, albeit hard-earned, lessons. And you're certainly wiser today than you were yesterday. So your suffering carries with it great potential: the potential for intense personal growth and the potential to help others.

As you begin to reorganize your life, look for ways to use your experiences for the betterment of others. When you do, you can rest assured that the course of your recovery will depend upon how quickly you discover new people to help and new reasons to live. And as you move through and beyond your own particular tough times, be mindful of this fact: As a survivor, you will have countless opportunities to serve others. By serving others, you will bring glory to God and meaning to the hardships you've endured.

## SOMETHING TO REMEMBER

Sometimes, waiting faithfully for God's plan to unfold is more important than understanding God's plan. Ruth Bell Graham once said, "When I am dealing with an all-powerful, all-knowing God, I, as a mere mortal, must offer my petitions not only with persistence, but also with patience. Someday I'll know why." So even when you can't understand God's plans, you must trust Him and never lose faith!

## MORE FROM GOD'S WORD ABOUT GOD'S PLAN

*Who are those who fear the Lord? He will show them the path they should choose. They will live in prosperity, and their children will inherit the Promised Land.*

Psalm 25:12-13 NLT

*And we know that in all things God works for the good of those who love him, who have been called according to his purpose.*

Romans 8:28 NIV

*The steps of the Godly are directed by the Lord. He delights in every detail of their lives. Though they stumble, they will not fall, for the Lord holds them by the hand.*

Psalm 37:23-24 NLT

*It is God who works in you to will and to act according to his good purpose.*

Philippians 2:13 NIV

*He replied, "Every plant that My heavenly Father didn't plant will be uprooted."*

Matthew 15:13 HCSB

## MORE POWERFUL IDEAS ABOUT GOD'S PLAN

In all the old castles of England, there was a place called the keep. It was always the strongest and best protected place in the castle, and in it were hidden all who were weak and helpless and unable to defend themselves in times of danger. Shall we be afraid to hide ourselves in the keeping power of our Divine Keeper, who neither slumbers nor sleeps, and who has promised to preserve our going out and our coming in, from this time forth and even forever more?

Hannah Whitall Smith

Trials are medicines which our gracious and wise physician prescribes because we need them; and he proportions the frequency and weight of them to what the case requires. Let us trust in his skill and thank him for his prescription.

John Newton

On the darkest day of your life, God is still in charge. Take comfort in that.

Marie T. Freeman

When you are in the furnace, your Father keeps His eye on the clock and His hand on the thermostat. He knows just how much we can take.

Warren Wiersbe

Every misfortune, every failure, every loss may be transformed. God has the power to transform all misfortunes into "God-sends."

Mrs. Charles E. Cowman

Don't let circumstances distress you. Rather, look for the will of God for your life to be revealed in and through those circumstances.

Billy Graham

Each problem is a God-appointed instructor.

Charles Swindoll

Our loving God uses difficulty in our lives to burn away the sin of self and build faith and spiritual power.

Bill Bright

We can take great comfort that God never sleeps—so we can.

Dianna Booher

It has been the faith of the Son of God who loves me and gave Himself for me that has held me in the darkest valley and the hottest fires and the deepest waters.

Elisabeth Elliot

## QUESTIONS TO CONSIDER

Am I really seeking God's will for my life, or am I just going through the motions?

_____

_____

Since I believe that God has a plan for my life, do I believe that He can help me overcome tough times and bring something good out of my hardships?

_____

_____

Do I regularly ask God to reveal His plans to me, and when I pray, do I listen carefully for His response?

_____

_____

## A PRAYER FOR TODAY

_Dear Lord, even when I am discouraged, even when my heart is heavy, I will earnestly seek Your will for my life. You have a plan for me that I can never fully understand. But You understand. And I will trust You today, tomorrow, and forever. Amen_

# Day 2

# WHEN OLD MAN TROUBLE PAYS A VISIT

*When you pass through the waters, I will be with you;*
*and through the rivers, they shall not overflow you.*
*When you walk through the fire, you shall not be burned,*
*nor shall the flame scorch you. For I am the Lord your God,*
*The Holy One of Israel, your Savior.*

Isaiah 43:2-3 NKJV

## THE FOCUS FOR TODAY

When problems threaten to engulf us, we must do
what believers have always done, turn to the Lord for
encouragement and solace. As Psalm 46:1 states,
"God is our refuge and strength,
an ever-present help in trouble."

Shirley Dobson

As life here on earth unfolds, all of us encounter occasional disappointments and setbacks: Those occasional visits from Old Man Trouble are simply a fact of life, and none of us are exempt. When tough times arrive, we may be forced to rearrange our plans and our priorities. But even on our darkest days, we must remember that God's love remains constant.

The fact that we encounter adversity is not nearly so important as the way we choose to deal with it. When tough times arrive, we have a clear choice: we can begin the difficult work of tackling our troubles . . . or not. When we summon the courage to look Old Man Trouble squarely in the eye, he usually blinks. But, if we refuse to address our problems, even the smallest annoyances have a way of growing into king-sized catastrophes.

As believers, we know that God loves us and that He will protect us. In times of hardship, He will comfort us; in times of sorrow, He will dry our tears. When we are troubled or weak or sorrowful, God is always with us. We must build our lives on the rock that cannot be shaken: we must trust in God. And then, we must get on with the hard work of tackling our problems . . . because if we don't, who will? Or should?

## WHEN YOUR FAITH IS TESTED

Life is a tapestry of good days and difficult days, with good days predominating. During the good days, we are tempted to take our blessings for granted (a temptation that we must resist with all our might). But, during life's difficult days, we discover precisely what we're made of. And more importantly, we discover what our faith is made of.

Has your faith been put to the test yet? If so, then you know that with God's help, you can endure life's darker days. When your faith is put to the test, rest assured that God is perfectly willing—and always ready—to give you strength for the struggle.

### SOMETHING TO REMEMBER

If you're having tough times, don't hit the panic button and don't keep everything bottled up inside. Find a person you can really trust, and talk things over. A second opinion (or, for that matter, a third, fourth, or fifth opinion) is usually helpful.

## MORE FROM GOD'S WORD ABOUT ADVERSITY

*We also have joy with our troubles, because we know that these troubles produce patience. And patience produces character, and character produces hope.*

Romans 5:3-4 NCV

*You pulled me from the brink of death, my feet from the cliff-edge of doom. Now I stroll at leisure with God in the sunlit fields of life.*

Psalm 56:13 MSG

*Don't fret or worry, Instead of worrying, pray. Let petitions and praises shape your worries into prayers, letting God know your concerns. Before you know it, a sense of God's wholeness, everything coming together for good, will come and settle you down. It's wonderful what happens when Christ displaces worry at the center of your life.*

Philippians 4:6-7 MSG

*Come to Me, all you who labor and are heavy laden, and I will give you rest. Take My yoke upon you and learn from Me, for I am gentle and lowly in heart, and you will find rest for your souls. For My yoke is easy and My burden is light.*

Matthew 11:28-30 NKJV

## MORE POWERFUL IDEAS ABOUT ADVERSITY

A faith that hasn't been tested can't be trusted.

Adrian Rogers

It's a good thing to have all the props pulled out from under us occasionally. It gives us some sense of what rock is under our feet, and what is sand. It stops us from taking anything for granted.

Madeleine L'Engle

I believe that the Creator of this universe takes delight in turning the terrors and tragedies that come with living in this old, fallen domain of the devil and transforming them into something that strengthens our hope, tests our faith, and shows forth His glory.

Al Green

When we face an impossible situation, all self-reliance and self-confidence must melt away; we must be totally dependent on Him for the resources.

Anne Graham Lotz

If things are tough, remember that every flower that ever bloomed had to go through a whole lot of dirt to get there.

Barbara Johnson

Like Paul, we may bear thorns
so that we can discover
God's perfect sufficiency.

—

Beth Moore

## MORE POWERFUL IDEAS ABOUT ADVERSITY

Life is literally filled with God-appointed storms. These squalls surge across everyone's horizon. We all need them.

*Charles Swindoll*

When the train goes through a tunnel and the world becomes dark, do you jump out? Of course not. You sit still and trust the engineer to get you through.

*Corrie ten Boom*

When the winds are cold, and the days are long, and thy soul from care would hide, fly back, fly back, to thy Father then, and beneath His wings abide.

*Fanny Crosby*

A mighty fortress is our God, a bulwark never failing our helper He, amid the flood of mortal ills prevailing for still our ancient foe doth seek to work us woe His craft and power are great, armed with cruel hate, our earth is not His equal.

*Martin Luther*

It is true of every stinging experience of our lives: Jesus, and Jesus alone, can rescue us.

*Franklin Graham*

## QUESTIONS TO CONSIDER

When tough times arrive, am I willing to place my future in God's hands?

_____

_____

Am I willing to work hard to resolve my own problems, or do I expect other people to solve them for me?

_____

_____

When I face adversity, am I willing to talk things over with family, with trusted friends, and with God . . . or do I keep everything bottled up inside?

_____

_____

### A PRAYER FOR TODAY
_Lord, when I face the inevitable disappointments of life, give me perspective and faith. When I am discouraged, give me the strength to trust Your promises and follow Your will. Then, when I have done my best, Father, let me live with the assurance that You are firmly in control, and that Your love endures forever. Amen_

# Day 3

# NO PROBLEMS ARE TOO BIG FOR GOD

*Is anything too hard for the LORD?*
Genesis 18:14 KJV

## THE FOCUS FOR TODAY

The grace of God is sufficient for all our needs,
for every problem and for every difficulty,
for every broken heart, and for every human sorrow.
Peter Marshall

Here's a riddle: What is it that is too unimportant to pray about yet too big for God to handle? The answer, of course, is: "nothing." Yet sometimes, when the challenges of the day seem overwhelming, we may spend more time worrying about our troubles than praying about them. And, we may spend more time fretting about our problems than solving them. A far better strategy, of course, is to pray as if everything depended entirely upon God and to work as if everything depended entirely upon us.

Life is an exercise in problem-solving. The question is not whether we will encounter problems; the real question is how we will choose to address them. When it comes to solving the problems of everyday living, we often know precisely what needs to be done, but we may be slow in doing it—especially if what needs to be done is difficult or uncomfortable for us. So we put off till tomorrow what should be done today.

The words of Psalm 34 remind us that the Lord solves problems for "people who do what is right." And usually, "doing what is right" means doing the uncomfortable work of confronting our problems sooner rather than later. So with no further ado, let the problem-solving begin . . . now!

## DO SOMETHING TODAY

Perhaps your troubles are simply too big to solve in a single sitting. But just because you can't solve everything doesn't mean that you should do nothing. So today, as a favor to yourself and as a way of breaking the bonds of procrastination, do something to make your situation better. Even a small step in the right direction is still a step in the right direction. And a small step is far, far better than no step at all.

---

### SOMETHING TO REMEMBER

Problem-solving 101: When it comes to solving problems, work beats worry. Remember: It is better to fix than to fret.

---

## MORE FROM GOD'S WORD ABOUT PROBLEMS

*People who do what is right may have many problems, but the Lord will solve them all.*

Psalm 34:19 NCV

*For when the way is rough, your patience has a chance to grow. So let it grow, and don't try to squirm out of your problems.*

James 1:3-4 TLB

*When you pass through the waters, I will be with you; and through the rivers, they shall not overflow you. When you walk through the fire, you shall not be burned, nor shall the flame scorch you. For I am the Lord your God, The Holy One of Israel, your Savior.*

Isaiah 43:2-3 NKJV

*Come to me, all you who are weary and burdened, and I will give you rest. Take my yoke upon you and learn from me, for I am gentle and humble in heart, and you will find rest for your souls. For my yoke is easy and my burden is light.*

Matthew 11:28-30 NIV

*Be of good courage, and he shall strengthen your heart, all ye that hope in the LORD.*

Psalm 31:24 KJV

## MORE POWERFUL IDEAS ABOUT PROBLEMS

Trial and triumph are what God uses to scribble all over the pages of our lives. They are signs that He is using us, loving us, shaping us to His image, enjoying our companionship, delivering us from evil, and writing eternity into our hearts.

Barbara Johnson

Measure the size of the obstacles against the size of God.

Beth Moore

We must face today as children of tomorrow. We must meet the uncertainties of this world with the certainty of the world to come. To the pure in heart nothing really bad can happen . . . not death, but sin, should be our greatest fear.

A. W. Tozer

Troubles we bear trustfully can bring us a fresh vision of God and a new outlook on life, an outlook of peace and hope.

Billy Graham

God knows exactly how much you can take, and He will never permit you to reach a breaking point.

Barbara Johnson

## QUESTIONS TO CONSIDER

When I encounter difficulties, do I understand the importance of looking for solutions?

_____

_____

Have I formed the habit of tackling problems sooner rather than later?

_____

_____

When I encounter difficulties, do I work to solve the problems instead of worrying about them, or do I often worry more than I work?

_____

_____

## A PRAYER FOR TODAY

*Lord, sometimes my problems are simply too big for me, but they are never too big for You.*
*Let me turn my troubles over to You, Lord, and let me trust in You today and for all eternity. Amen*

## Day 4

# TOUGH TIMES BUILD CHARACTER

*People with integrity have firm footing,*
*but those who follow crooked paths will slip and fall.*
Proverbs 10:9 NLT


## THE FOCUS FOR TODAY

Character is both developed and revealed by tests,
and all of life is a test.
Rick Warren

Psalm 145 promises, "The Lord is near to all who call on him, to all who call on him in truth. He fulfills the desires of those who fear him; he hears their cry and saves them" (vv. 18-20 NIV). And the words of Jesus offer us comfort: "These things I have spoken to you, that in Me you may have peace. In the world you will have tribulation; but be of good cheer, I have overcome the world" (John 16:33 NKJV).

The times that try your soul are also the times that build your character. During the darker days of life, you can learn lessons that are impossible to learn during sunny, happier days. Times of adversity can—and should—be times of intense spiritual and personal growth. But God will not force you to learn the lessons of adversity. You must learn them for yourself.

## DO THE HARD THING FIRST

The habit of putting things off until the last minute, along with its first cousin, the habit of making excuses for work that was never done, can be detrimental to your life and to your character.

Are you in the habit of doing what needs to be done when it needs to be done, or are you a dues-paying member of the Procrastinator's Club? If you've acquired the habit of doing things sooner rather than later, congratulations! But, if you find yourself putting off all those unpleasant tasks until later (or never), it's time to think about the consequences of your behavior.

One way that you can learn to defeat procrastination is by paying less attention to your fears and more attention to your responsibilities. So, when you're faced with a difficult choice or an unpleasant responsibility, don't spend endless hours fretting over your fate. Simply seek God's counsel and get busy. When you do, you will be richly rewarded because of your willingness to act.

---

## SOMETHING TO REMEMBER

Perhaps, because of tough times, you're being forced to step outside your comfort zone. If so, consider it an opportunity to grow spiritually and emotionally. Your challenge is to believe in yourself, to trust God, and to follow God's lead, even if He leads you outside your comfort zone.

---

## MORE FROM GOD'S WORD ABOUT CHARACTER

*Do not be misled: "Bad company corrupts good character."*

1 Corinthians 15:33 NIV

*Applying all diligence, in your faith supply moral excellence.*

2 Peter 1:5 NASB

*The righteousness of the blameless clears his path, but the wicked person will fall because of his wickedness.*

Proverbs 11:5 HCSB

*A good name is more desirable than great riches; to be esteemed is better than silver or gold.*

Proverbs 22:1 NIV

*We also have joy with our troubles, because we know that these troubles produce patience. And patience produces character, and character produces hope.*

Romans 5:3-4 NCV

## MORE POWERFUL IDEAS ABOUT CHARACTER

Every time you refuse to face up to life and its problems, you weaken your character.

E. Stanley Jones

Character cannot be developed in ease and quiet. Only through experience of trial and suffering can the soul be strengthened, vision cleared, ambition inspired, and success achieved.

Helen Keller

Let God use times of waiting to mold and shape your character. Let God use those times to purify your life and make you into a clean vessel for His service.

Henry Blackaby and Claude King

Character is what you are in the dark.

D. L. Moody

Often, our character is at greater risk in prosperity than in adversity.

Beth Moore

Jesus—the standard of measurement, the scale of weights, the test of character for the whole moral universe.

R. G. Lee

## QUESTIONS TO CONSIDER

Do I believe that tough times can build (or can reveal) character?

_____

_____

Am I determined to learn the lessons that tough times have to teach?

_____

_____

Even when times are tough, do I refuse to compromise my character?

_____

_____

## A PRAYER FOR TODAY

_Dear Lord, every day can be an exercise in character-building, and that's what I intend to make this day. I will be mindful that my thoughts and actions have great consequences in my own life and in the lives of my loved ones. I will strive to make my thoughts and actions pleasing to You, so that I may be an instrument of Your peace every day. Amen_

# Day 5

# THE LESSONS OF ADVERSITY

*He heals the brokenhearted and bandages their wounds.*

Psalm 147:3 NCV

## THE FOCUS FOR TODAY

God's curriculum for all who sincerely want to know Him and do His will always includes lessons we wish we could skip. With an intimate understanding of our deepest needs and individual capacities, He chooses our curriculum.

Elisabeth Elliot

Whether you're twenty-two or a hundred and two, you've still got lots to learn. Even if you're very wise, God isn't finished with you yet, and He isn't finished teaching you important lessons about life here on earth and life eternal.

God does not intend for you to remain stuck in one place. Far from it! God wants you to continue growing as a person and as a Christian every day that you live. And make no mistake: both spiritual and intellectual growth are possible during every stage of life—during the happiest days or the hardest ones.

How can you make sure that you'll keep growing (and learning) during good times and hard times? You do so through prayer, through worship, through fellowship, through an openness to God's Holy Spirit, and through a careful study of God's Holy Word.

Your Bible contains powerful prescriptions for overcoming tough times. When you study God's Word and live according to His commandments, adversity becomes a practical instructor. While you're enduring difficult days, you learn lessons you simply could not have learned any other way. And when you learn those lessons, you will serve as a shining example to your friends, to your family, and to the world.

## OLD MAN TROUBLE HAS LESSONS TO TEACH

The next time Old Man Trouble knocks on your door, remember that he has lessons to teach. So turn away Mr. Trouble as quickly as you can, but as you're doing so, don't forget to learn his lessons. And remember: the trouble with trouble isn't just the trouble it causes; it's also the trouble we cause ourselves if we ignore the things that trouble has to teach. Got that? Then please don't forget it!

---

### SOMETHING TO REMEMBER

Talk about it! If you're having tough times, don't hit the panic button and don't keep everything bottled up inside. Talk things over with people you can really trust. And if your troubles seem overwhelming, be willing to seek help—starting, of course, with your family and your pastor.

---

## MORE FROM GOD'S WORD ABOUT WISDOM

*The Lord says, "I will make you wise and show you where to go. I will guide you and watch over you."*

Psalm 32:8 NCV

*Wisdom is the principal thing; therefore get wisdom. And in all your getting, get understanding.*

Proverbs 4:7 NKJV

*Happy is the person who finds wisdom, the one who gets understanding.*

Proverbs 3:13 NCV

*Anyone who listens to my teaching and obeys me is wise, like a person who builds a house on solid rock. Though the rain comes in torrents and the floodwaters rise and the winds beat against that house, it won't collapse, because it is built on rock.*

Matthew 7:24–25 NLT

*But the wisdom that is from above is first pure, then peaceable, gentle, willing to yield, full of mercy and good fruits, without partiality and without hypocrisy.*

James 3:17 NKJV

## MORE POWERFUL IDEAS ABOUT WISDOM

God allows us to experience the low points of life in order to teach us lessons that we could learn in no other way.

C. S. Lewis

If your every human plan and calculation has miscarried, if, one by one, human props have been knocked out, take heart. God is trying to get a message through to you, and the message is: "Stop depending on inadequate human resources. Let me handle the matter."

Catherine Marshall

Life is literally filled with God-appointed storms. These squalls surge across everyone's horizon. We all need them.

Charles Swindoll

While chastening is always difficult, if we look to God for the lesson we should learn, we will see spiritual fruit.

Vonette Bright

Recently I've been learning that life comes down to this: God is in everything. Regardless of what difficulties I am experiencing at the moment, or what things aren't as I would like them to be, I look at the circumstances and say, "Lord, what are you trying to teach me?"

Catherine Marshall

## QUESTIONS TO CONSIDER

Do I understand the importance of seeking God's wisdom and His guidance?

_____

_____

Do I allow God to guide me by His Word and by His Spirit?

_____

_____

Do I understand that God still has important lessons to teach me?

_____

_____

### A PRAYER FOR TODAY
_Dear Lord, I have so much to learn._
_Help me to watch, to listen, to think, and to learn,_
_every day of my life. Amen_

# Day 6

# ACCEPTING ADVICE

*A wise man will hear and increase learning,*
*and a man of understanding will attain wise counsel.*
Proverbs 1:5 NKJV

## THE FOCUS FOR TODAY

It takes a wise person to give good advice,
but an even wiser person to take it.
Marie T. Freeman

I f you find yourself caught up in a difficult situation, it's time to start searching for knowledgeable friends and mentors who can give you solid advice. Why do you need help evaluating the person in the mirror? Because you're simply too close to that person, that's why. Sometimes, you'll be tempted to give yourself straight A's when you deserve considerably lower grades. On other occasions, you'll become your own worst critic, giving yourself a string of failing marks when you deserve better. The truth, of course, is often somewhere in the middle.

Finding a wise mentor is only half the battle. It takes just as much wisdom—and sometimes more—to act upon good advice as it does to give it. So find people you can trust, listen to them carefully, and act accordingly.

## FIND A MENTOR

If you're going through tough times, it's helpful to find mentors who have been there, and done that—people who have experienced your particular challenge and lived to tell about it.

When you find mentors who are godly men and women, you become a more godly person yourself. That's why you should seek out advisers who, by their words and their presence, make you a better person and a better Christian.

Today, as a gift to yourself, select, from your friends and family members, a mentor whose judgment you trust. Then listen carefully to your mentor's advice and be willing to accept that advice, even if accepting it requires effort or pain, or both. Consider your mentor to be God's gift to you. Thank God for that gift, and use it for the glory of His kingdom.

---

### SOMETHING TO REMEMBER

If you can't seem to listen to constructive criticism with an open mind, perhaps you've got a severe case of old-fashioned stubbornness. If so, ask God to soften your heart, open your ears, and enlighten your mind.

### MORE FROM GOD'S WORD ABOUT ACCEPTING ADVICE

*He is God. Let him do whatever he thinks best.*

1 Samuel 3:18 MSG

*It is better to be a poor but wise youth than to be an old and foolish king who refuses all advice.*

Ecclesiastes 4:13 NLT

*It is better to listen to rebuke from a wise person than to listen to the song of fools.*

Ecclesiastes 7:5 HCSB

*Know-it-alls don't like being told what to do; they avoid the company of wise men and women.*

Proverbs 15:12 MSG

*Listen to counsel and receive instruction so that you may be wise in later life.*

Proverbs 19:20 HCSB

## MORE POWERFUL IDEAS ABOUT MENTORS

God guides through the counsel of good people.

E. Stanley Jones

A single word, if spoken in a friendly spirit, may be sufficient to turn one from dangerous error.

Fanny Crosby

No matter how crazy or nutty your life has seemed, God can make something strong and good out of it. He can help you grow wide branches for others to use as shelter.

Barbara Johnson

God often keeps us on the path by guiding us through the counsel of friends and trusted spiritual advisors.

Bill Hybels

Do not open your heart to every man, but discuss your affairs with one who is wise and who fears God.

Thomas à Kempis

Yes, the Spirit was sent to be our Counselor. Yes, Jesus speaks to us personally. But often he works through another human being.

John Eldredge

## QUESTIONS TO CONSIDER

Do I understand the importance of finding—and listening to—mentors?

_____

_____

Am I willing to be a mentor to others?

_____

_____

Am I willing to listen carefully to advice and, when appropriate, to take it? Or am I a little too stubborn to take advice from others?

_____

_____

## A PRAYER FOR TODAY

_Dear Lord, thank You for the mentors whom You have placed along my path. When I am troubled, let me turn to them for help, for guidance, for comfort, and for perspective. And Father, let me be a friend and mentor to others, so that my love for You may be demonstrated by my genuine concern for them. Amen_

# Day 7

# FAITH MOVES MOUNTAINS

*For whatever is born of God overcomes the world.*
*And this is the victory that has overcome the world—*
*our faith.*

1 John 5:4 NKJV

## THE FOCUS FOR TODAY

Trials are not enemies of faith but opportunities
to reveal God's faithfulness.

Barbara Johnson

Every life—including yours—is a grand adventure made great by faith. Every step of the way, through every triumph and tragedy, God will stand by your side and strengthen you . . . if you have faith in Him.

Job had every opportunity to give up on himself and to give up on God. But despite his suffering, Job refused to curse his Creator. Job trusted God in the darkest moments of his life, and so did Jesus.

Before His crucifixion, Jesus went to the Mount of Olives and poured out His heart to God (Luke 22). Jesus knew of the agony that He was destined to endure, but He also knew that God's will must be done. We, like our Savior, face trials that bring fear and trembling to the very depths of our souls, but like Jesus, we should seek God's will, not our own.

When you entrust your life to God completely and without reservation, He will give you the strength to meet any challenge, the courage to face any trial, and the wisdom to live in His righteousness and in His peace. So strengthen your faith through praise, through worship, through Bible study, and through prayer. And trust God's plans. With Him, all things are possible, and He stands ready to open a world of possibilities to you . . . if you have faith.

## NOURISH YOUR FAITH

When we trust God, we should trust Him without reservation. But sometimes, especially during life's darker days, trusting God may be difficult. Yet this much is certain: whatever our circumstances, we must continue to plant the seeds of faith in our hearts, trusting that in time, God will bring forth a bountiful harvest. Planting the seeds for that harvest requires work, which is perfectly okay with God. After all, He never gives us burdens that we cannot bear.

It is important to remember that the work required to build and sustain our faith is an ongoing process. Corrie ten Boom advised, "Be filled with the Holy Spirit; join a church where the members believe the Bible and know the Lord; seek the fellowship of other Christians; learn and be nourished by God's Word and His many promises. Conversion is not the end of your journey—it is only the beginning."

The work of nourishing your faith can and should be joyful work. The hours that you invest in Bible study, prayer, meditation, and worship should be times of enrichment and celebration. And, as you continue to build your life upon a foundation of faith, you will discover that the journey toward spiritual maturity lasts a lifetime. As a child of God, you are never fully "grown." Instead, you can continue "growing up" every day of your life. And that's exactly what God wants you to do.

---

SOMETHING TO REMEMBER

Feelings come and go, but God never changes. So when you have a choice between trusting your feelings or trusting God, trust God. And remember that if your faith is strong enough, you and God—working together—can move mountains.

---

## MORE FROM GOD'S WORD ABOUT FAITH

*Be on the alert, stand firm in the faith, act like men, be strong.*

1 Corinthians 16:13 NASB

*It is impossible to please God apart from faith. And why? Because anyone who wants to approach God must believe both that he exists and that he cares enough to respond to those who seek him.*

Hebrews 11:6 MSG

## MORE POWERFUL IDEAS ABOUT FAITH

It may be the most difficult time of your life. You may be enduring your own whirlwind. But the whirlwind is a temporary experience. Your faithful, caring Lord will see you through.

Charles Swindoll

I am truly grateful that faith enables me to move past the question of "Why?"

Zig Ziglar

When you enroll in the "school of faith," you never know what may happen next. The life of faith presents challenges that keep you going—and keep you growing!

Warren Wiersbe

Nothing is more disastrous than to study faith, analyze faith, make noble resolves of faith, but never actually to make the leap of faith.

Vance Havner

Faith is our spiritual oxygen. It not only keeps us alive in God, but enables us to grow stronger . . . .

Joyce Landorf Heatherly

## QUESTIONS TO CONSIDER

Am I willing to ask God to become a full partner in my life?

_____

_____

Am I willing to pray as if everything depended upon God and work as if everything depended upon me?

_____

_____

After I've done my best, am I willing to trust God's plan and His timetable for my life?

_____

_____

### A PRAYER FOR TODAY

_Lord, sometimes this world is a terrifying place._
_When I am filled with uncertainty and doubt, give me_
_faith. In life's dark moments, help me remember_
_that You are always near and that You can overcome_
_any challenge. Today, Lord, and forever,_
_I will place my trust in You. Amen_

# Day 8

# THE RIGHT KIND
# OF ATTITUDE

*For God has not given us a spirit of fearfulness,*
*but one of power, love, and sound judgment.*

2 Timothy 1:7 HCSB

## THE FOCUS FOR TODAY

We are either the masters or the victims of our attitudes.
It is a matter of personal choice. Who we are today
is the result of choices we made yesterday.
Tomorrow, we will become what we choose today.
To change means to choose to change.

John Maxwell

If you want to defeat Old Man Trouble, you'll need the right kind of attitude: the positive kind. So what's your attitude today? Are you fearful, angry, bored, or worried? Are you pessimistic, perplexed, pained, and perturbed? Are you moping around with a frown on your face that's almost as big as the one in your heart? If so, God wants to have a little talk with you.

God created you in His own image, and He wants you to experience joy, contentment, peace, and abundance. But, God will not force you to experience these things; you must claim them for yourself.

God has given you free will, including the ability to influence the direction and the tone of your thoughts. And, here's how God wants you to direct those thoughts:
"

*Finally brothers, whatever is true, whatever is honorable, whatever is just, whatever is pure, whatever is lovely, whatever is commendable—if there is any moral excellence and if there is any praise—dwell on these things*" (Philippians 4:8 HCSB).

The quality of your attitude will help determine the quality of your life, so you must guard your thoughts accordingly. If you make up your mind to approach life with a healthy mixture of realism and optimism, you'll be rewarded. But, if you allow yourself to fall into the unfortunate habit of negative thinking, you will doom yourself to unhappiness or mediocrity, or worse.

So, the next time you find yourself dwelling upon the negative aspects of your life, refocus your attention on things positive. The next time you find yourself falling prey to the blight of pessimism, stop yourself and turn your thoughts around. The next time you're tempted to waste valuable time gossiping or complaining, resist those temptations with all your might.

And remember: You'll never whine your way to the top . . . so don't waste your breath.

---

### SOMETHING TO REMEMBER

A positive attitude leads to positive results; a negative attitude leads elsewhere. And if you want to improve the quality of your thoughts, ask God to help you.

---

## MORE FROM GOD'S WORD ABOUT YOUR ATTITUDE

*Set your mind on things above, not on things on the earth.*

Colossians 3:2 NKJV

*Come near to God, and God will come near to you. You sinners, clean sin out of your lives. You who are trying to follow God and the world at the same time, make your thinking pure.*

James 4:8 NCV

*Those who are pure in their thinking are happy, because they will be with God.*

Matthew 5:8 NCV

*Finally, brethren, whatever is true, whatever is honorable, whatever is right, whatever is pure, whatever is lovely, whatever is of good repute, if there is any excellence and if anything worthy of praise, dwell on these things.*

Philippians 4:8 NASB

*So prepare your minds for service and have self-control.*

1 Peter 1:13 NCV

## MORE POWERFUL IDEAS ABOUT YOUR ATTITUDE

We shouldn't deny the pain of what happens in our lives. But, we should refuse to focus only on the valleys.

Charles Swindoll

Attitude is more important than the past, than education, than money, than circumstances, than what people do or say. It is more important than appearance, giftedness, or skill.

Charles Swindoll

The mind is like a clock that is constantly running down. It has to be wound up daily with good thoughts.

Fulton J. Sheen

The difference between winning and losing is how we choose to react to disappointment.

Barbara Johnson

It's your choice: you can either count your blessings or recount your disappointments.

Jim Gallery

Pain is inevitable, but misery is optional.

Max Lucado

## QUESTIONS TO CONSIDER

Do I associate with people who are upbeat, optimistic, and encouraging?

_____

_____

Do I try to focus more on my blessings and less on my hardships?

_____

_____

Have I trained myself to look for possibilities, not obstacles?

_____

_____

### A PRAYER FOR TODAY
*Lord, I pray for an attitude that is Christlike.*
*Whatever my circumstances, whether good or bad,*
*triumphal or tragic, let my response reflect*
*a God-honoring attitude of optimism, faith,*
*and love for You. Amen*

# Day 9

# TRUSTING GOD'S TIMING

*I waited patiently for the LORD;*
*And He inclined to me, and heard my cry.*

Psalm 40:1 NKJV

## THE FOCUS FOR TODAY

Will not the Lord's time be better than your time?

C. H. Spurgeon

The Bible teaches us to trust God's timing in all matters, but we are sorely tempted to do otherwise, especially when times are tough. When we are beset with problems, we are understandably anxious for a quick conclusion to our hardships. We know that our problems will end some day, and we want it to end NOW. God, however, works on His own timetable, and His schedule does not always coincide with ours.

God's plans are perfect; ours most certainly are not. So we must learn to trust the Father in good times and hard times. No exceptions.

Elisabeth Elliot advised, "We must learn to move according to the timetable of the Timeless One, and to be at peace." And Billy Graham observed, "As we wait on God, He helps us use the winds of adversity to soar above our problems."

So today, as you meet the challenges of everyday life, do your best to turn everything over to God. Whatever "it" is, He can handle it. And you can be sure that He will handle it when the time is right.

## PRAY FOR PATIENCE

Would you like to become a more patient person? Pray about it. Is there a person you dislike? Pray for a forgiving heart. Do you lose your temper more than you should? Ask God for help. Are you mired in the quicksand of regret? Ask God to liberate you.

As you pray more, you'll discover that God is always near and that He's always ready to hear from you. So don't worry about things; pray about them. God is waiting . . . and listening!

---

### SOMETHING TO REMEMBER

God is in control of His world and your world. Rely upon Him. Vance Havner writes, "When we get to a place where it can't be done unless God does it, God will do it!" Enough said.

## MORE FROM GOD'S WORD ABOUT GOD'S TIMING

*Humble yourselves, therefore, under God's mighty hand, that he may lift you up in due time.*

1 Peter 5:6 NIV

*He told them, "You don't get to know the time. Timing is the Father's business."*

Acts 1:7 MSG

*From one man he made every nation of men, that they should inhabit the whole earth; and he determined the times set for them and the exact places where they should live.*

Acts 17:26 NIV

*There is a time for everything, and a season for every activity under heaven.*

Ecclesiastes 3:1 NIV

*Yet the LORD longs to be gracious to you; he rises to show you compassion. For the LORD is a God of justice. Blessed are all who wait for him!*

Isaiah 30:18 NIV

## MORE POWERFUL IDEAS ABOUT GOD'S TIMING

By his wisdom, he orders his delays so that they prove to be far better than our hurries.

C. H. Spurgeon

God is in no hurry. Compared to the works of mankind, He is extremely deliberate. God is not a slave to the human clock.

Charles Swindoll

When we read of the great Biblical leaders, we see that it was not uncommon for God to ask them to wait, not just a day or two, but for years, until God was ready for them to act.

Gloria Gaither

We must leave it to God to answer our prayers in His own wisest way. Sometimes, we are so impatient and think that God does not answer. God always answers! He never fails! Be still. Abide in Him.

Mrs. Charles E. Cowman

Our challenge is to wait in faith for the day of God's favor and salvation.

Jim Cymbala

## QUESTIONS TO CONSIDER

Do I take seriously the Bible's instructions to be patient?

_____

_____

Do I believe that patience is not idle waiting but that it is an activity that means watching and waiting for God to lead me in the direction of His choosing?

_____

_____

Even when I don't understand the circumstances that confront me, do I strive to wait patiently while serving the Lord?

_____

_____

### A PRAYER FOR TODAY
_Dear Lord, Your timing is seldom my timing, but Your timing is always right for me. You are my Father, and You have a plan for my life that is grander than I can imagine. When I am impatient, remind me that You are never early or late. You are always on time, Lord, so let me trust in You . . . always. Amen_

# Day 10

# ASK HIM

*So I say to you, keep asking, and it will be given to you.*
*Keep searching, and you will find.*
*Keep knocking, and the door will be opened to you.*
Luke 11:9 HCSB

## THE FOCUS FOR TODAY

God will help us become the people we are meant to be,
if only we will ask Him.
Hannah Whitall Smith

How often do you ask God for His help and His wisdom? Occasionally? Intermittently? Whenever you experience a crisis? Hopefully not. Hopefully, you've acquired the habit of asking for God's assistance early and often. And hopefully, you have learned to seek His guidance in every aspect of your life.

Jesus made it clear to His disciples: they should petition God to meet their needs. So should you. Genuine, heartfelt prayer produces powerful changes in you and in your world. When you lift your heart to God, you open yourself to a never-ending source of divine wisdom and infinite love.

James 5:16 makes a promise that God intends to keep: when you pray earnestly, fervently, and often, great things will happen. Too many people, however, are too timid or too pessimistic to ask God to do big things. Please don't count yourself among their number.

God can do great things through you if you have the courage to ask Him (and the determination to keep asking Him). But don't expect Him to do all the work. When you do your part, He will do His part—and when He does, you can expect miracles to happen.

The Bible promises that God will guide you if you let Him. Your job is to let Him. But sometimes, you will be tempted to do otherwise. Sometimes, you'll be tempted to go along with the crowd; other times, you'll be tempted to do things your way, not God's way. When you feel those temptations, resist them.

God has promised that when you ask for His help, He will not withhold it. So ask. Ask Him to meet the needs of your day. Ask Him to lead you, to protect you, and to correct you. Then, trust the answers He gives.

God stands at the door and waits. When you knock, He opens. When you ask, He answers. Your task, of course, is to make God a full partner in every aspect of your life—in good times and in hard times—and to seek His guidance prayerfully, confidently, and often.

---

### SOMETHING TO REMEMBER

When you ask God for His assistance, He hears your request—and in His own time, He answers. If you need more, ask more.

---

## MORE FROM GOD'S WORD ABOUT ASKING GOD FOR THE THINGS YOU NEED

*If you need wisdom—if you want to know what God wants you to do—ask him, and he will gladly tell you. He will not resent your asking.*

James 1:5 NLT

*From now on, whatever you request along the lines of who I am and what I am doing, I'll do it. That's how the Father will be seen for who he is in the Son. I mean it. Whatever you request in this way, I'll do.*

John 14:13-14 MSG

*You did not choose me, but I chose you and appointed you to go and bear fruit—fruit that will last. Then the Father will give you whatever you ask in my name.*

John 15:16 NIV

*You fathers—if your children ask for a fish, do you give them a snake instead? Or if they ask for an egg, do you give them a scorpion? Of course not! If you sinful people know how to give good gifts to your children, how much more will your heavenly Father give the Holy Spirit to those who ask him.*

Luke 11:11-13 NLT

## MORE POWERFUL IDEAS ABOUT ASKING GOD

We sometimes fear to bring our troubles to God, because they must seem so small to him who sitteth on the circle of the earth. But, if they are large enough to vex and endanger our welfare, they are large enough to touch his heart of love.

R. A. Torrey

When will we realize that we're not troubling God with our questions and concerns? His heart is open to hear us—his touch nearer than our next thought—as if no one in the world existed but us. Our very personal God wants to hear from us personally.

Gigi Graham Tchividjian

All we have to do is to acknowledge our need, move from self-sufficiency to dependence, and ask God to become our hiding place.

Bill Hybels

Some people think God does not like to be troubled with our constant asking. But, the way to trouble God is not to come at all.

D. L. Moody

## QUESTIONS TO CONSIDER

When I need more from life, do I ask more from God?

_____

_____

When I want to achieve a worthy goal, do I ask for God's help—and keep asking—until He answers my prayers?

_____

_____

Have I acquired the habit of asking for God's help many times each day?

_____

_____

### A PRAYER FOR TODAY

_Dear Lord, when I have questions or fears, I will turn to You. When I am weak, I will seek Your strength. When I am discouraged, Father, I will be mindful of Your love and Your grace. I will ask You for the things I need, Father, and I will trust Your answers, today and forever. Amen_

# Day 11

# FINALLY MAKING PEACE WITH THE PAST

*Peace I leave with you, my peace I give unto you:*
*not as the world giveth, give I unto you.*
*Let not your heart be troubled, neither let it be afraid.*

John 14:27 KJV

## THE FOCUS FOR TODAY

If you are God's child, you are no longer bound
to your past or to what you were.
You are a brand new creature in Christ Jesus.

Kay Arthur

Some of life's greatest roadblocks are not the ones we see through the windshield; they are, instead, the roadblocks that seem to fill the rearview mirror. Because we are imperfect human beings who lack perfect control over our thoughts, we may allow ourselves to become "stuck" in the past—even though we know better. Instead of focusing our thoughts and energies on the opportunities of today, we may allow painful memories to fill our minds and sap our strength. We simply can't seem to let go of our pain, so we relive it again and again . . . with predictably unfortunate consequences. Thankfully, God has other plans.

Philippians 3:13-14 instructs us to focus on the future, not the past: "One thing I do, forgetting those things which are behind and reaching forward to those things which are ahead, I press toward the goal for the prize of the upward call of God in Christ Jesus" (NKJV). Yet for many of us, focusing on the future is difficult indeed. Why? Part of the problem has to do with forgiveness. When we find ourselves focusing too intently on the past, it's a sure sign that we need to focus, instead, on a more urgent need: the need to forgive.

Focusing too intently on the past is, almost without exception, futile. No amount of anger or bitterness can change what happened yesterday. Tears can't change the past; regrets can't change it. Our worries won't change the past, and neither will our complaints. Simply put, the past is, and always will be, the past. Forever.

Can you summon both the courage and the wisdom to accept your past and move on with your life? Can you accept the reality that yesterday—and all the yesterdays before it—are gone? And, can you entrust all those yesterdays to God? Hopefully you can.

Once you have made peace with your past, you are free to become fully engaged in the present. And when you become fully engaged in the present, you are then free to build a better future for yourself and your loved ones.

If you've endured a difficult past, learn from it, but don't live in it. Instead, build your future on a firm foundation of trust and forgiveness: trust in your Heavenly Father, and forgiveness for all His children, including yourself. Give all your yesterdays to God, and celebrate this day with hope in your heart and praise on your lips. Your Creator intends to use you in wonderful, unexpected ways if you let Him. But first, God wants you to make peace with your past . . . and He wants you to do it now.

---

SOMETHING TO REMEMBER

The past is past, so don't invest all your energy there.

---

## MORE FROM GOD'S WORD ABOUT THE PAST

*Do not remember the past events, pay no attention to things of old. Look, I am about to do something new; even now it is coming. Do you not see it? Indeed, I will make a way in the wilderness, rivers in the desert.*

Isaiah 43:18-19 HCSB

*I do not consider myself yet to have taken hold of it. But one thing I do: Forgetting what is behind and straining toward what is ahead, I press on toward the goal to win the prize for which God has called me heavenward in Christ Jesus.*

Philippians 3:13-14 NIV

*Create in me a pure heart, O God, and renew a steadfast spirit within me.*

Psalm 51:10 NIV

*And He who sits on the throne said, "Behold, I am making all things new."*

Revelation 21:5 NASB

*Your old life is dead. Your new life, which is your real life— even though invisible to spectators—is with Christ in God. He is your life.*

Colossians 3:3 MSG

## MORE POWERFUL IDEAS ABOUT THE PAST

Our yesterdays present irreparable things to us; it is true that we have lost opportunities which will never return, but God can transform this destructive anxiety into a constructive thoughtfulness for the future. Let the past sleep, but let it sleep on the bosom of Christ. Leave the Irreparable Past in His hands, and step out into the Irresistible Future with Him.

Oswald Chambers

Shake the dust from your past, and move forward in His promises.

Kay Arthur

Our yesterdays teach us how to savor our todays and tomorrows.

Patsy Clairmont

We set our eyes on the finish line, forgetting the past, and straining toward the mark of spiritual maturity and fruitfulness.

Vonette Bright

Not the power to remember, but its very opposite, the power to forget, is a necessary condition for our existence.

St. Basil

## MORE POWERFUL IDEAS ABOUT ACCEPTANCE

Tomorrow's job is fathered by today's acceptance. Acceptance of what, at least for the moment, you cannot alter.

*Max Lucado*

It is always possible to do the will of God. In every place and time it is within our power to acquiesce in the will of God.

*Elisabeth Elliot*

We must meet our disappointments, our persecutions, our malicious enemies, our provoking friends, our trials and temptations of every sort, with an attitude of surrender and trust. We must spread our wings and "mount up" to the "heavenly places in Christ" above them all, where they will lose their power to harm or distress us.

*Hannah Whitall Smith*

Acceptance says: True, this is my situation at the moment. I'll look unblinkingly at the reality of it. But, I'll also open my hands to accept willingly whatever a loving Father sends me.

*Catherine Marshall*

Two words will help you cope
when you run low on hope:
accept and trust.

—

Charles Swindoll

## QUESTIONS TO CONSIDER

Am I able to learn from the past and accept the past, but live in the present?

_____

_____

Do I believe that it is important to trust God even when I don't understand why certain things happen?

_____

_____

Am I willing to change the things I can change and accept the things I can't?

_____

_____

### A PRAYER FOR TODAY

*Heavenly Father, free me from anger, resentment, and envy. When I am bitter, I cannot feel the peace that You intend for my life. Keep me mindful that forgiveness is Your commandment, and help me accept the past, treasure the present, and trust the future . . . to You. Amen*

# Day 12

# THE POWER OF PRAYER

*Is anyone among you suffering? He should pray.*
*Is anyone cheerful? He should sing praises.*
James 5:13 HCSB

## THE FOCUS FOR TODAY

I have found the perfect antidote for fear.
Whenever it sticks up its ugly face,
I clobber it with prayer.

Dale Evans Rogers

God is trying to get His message through . . . to you! Are you listening?

Perhaps, if you're experiencing tough times, you may find yourself overwhelmed by the press of everyday life. Perhaps you forget to slow yourself down long enough to talk with God. Instead of turning your thoughts and prayers to Him, you may rely upon your own resources. Instead of asking God for guidance, you may depend only upon your own limited wisdom. A far better course of action is this: simply stop what you're doing long enough to open your heart to God; then listen carefully for His directions.

Do you spend time each day with God? You should. Are you in need? Ask God to sustain you. Are you troubled? Take your worries to Him in prayer. Are you weary? Seek God's strength. In all things great and small, seek God's wisdom and His grace. He hears your prayers, and He will answer. All you must do is ask.

## GOT QUESTIONS?

You've got questions? God's got answers. And if you'd like to hear from Him, here's precisely what you must do: petition Him with a sincere heart; be still; be patient; and listen. Then, in His own time and in His own fashion,

God will answer your questions and give you guidance for the journey ahead.

Today, turn over everything to your Creator. Pray constantly about matters great and small. Seek God's instruction and His direction. And remember: God hears your prayers and answers them. But He won't answer the prayers that you don't get around to praying. So pray early and often. And then wait patiently for answers that are sure to come.

---

### SOMETHING TO REMEMBER

Sometimes, the answer is "No." God does not answer all of our prayers in the affirmative, nor should He. His job is not to grant all our earthly requests; His job is to offer us eternal salvation (for which we must be eternally grateful). When we are disappointed by the realities of life-here-on-earth, we should remember that our prayers are always answered by a sovereign, all-knowing God, and that we must trust Him, whether He answers "Yes," "No," or "Not yet."

---

## MORE FROM GOD'S WORD ABOUT PRAYER

*"Relax, Daniel," he continued, "don't be afraid. From the moment you decided to humble yourself to receive understanding, your prayer was heard, and I set out to come to you."*

Daniel 10:12 MSG

*If you don't know what you're doing, pray to the Father. He loves to help. You'll get his help, and won't be condescended to when you ask for it. Ask boldly, believingly, without a second thought. People who "worry their prayers" are like wind-whipped waves. Don't think you're going to get anything from the Master that way, adrift at sea, keeping all your options open.*

James 1:5-8 MSG

*Rejoice always, pray without ceasing, in everything give thanks; for this is the will of God in Christ Jesus for you.*

1 Thessalonians 5:16-18 NKJV

*If my people who are called by my name, will humble themselves and pray and seek my face and turn from their wicked ways, then will I hear from heaven and will forgive their sin and will heal their land.*

2 Chronicles 7:14 NIV

## MORE POWERFUL IDEAS ABOUT PRAYER

God always answers the prayers of His children—but His answer isn't always "Yes."

Billy Graham

I have witnessed many attitudes make a positive turnaround through prayer.

John Maxwell

Real power in prayer flows only when a man's spirit touches God's spirit.

Catherine Marshall

Any concern that is too small to be turned into a prayer is too small to be made into a burden.

Corrie ten Boom

When we pray, we have linked ourselves with Divine purposes, and we therefore have Divine power at our disposal for human living.

E. Stanley Jones

Prayer accomplishes more than anything else.

Bill Bright

## QUESTIONS TO CONSIDER

Do I understand that prayer strengthens my relationship with God?

_____

_____

Do I trust that God will care for me, even when it seems that my prayers have gone unanswered?

_____

_____

Do I believe that my prayers have the power to change my circumstances, my perspective, and my future?

_____

_____

## A PRAYER FOR TODAY

*Dear Lord, let me raise my hopes and my dreams,
my worries and my fears to You. Let me be a worthy
example to family and friends, showing them the
importance and the power of prayer. Let me take
everything to You in prayer, Lord, and when I do,
let me trust in Your answers. Amen*

# Day 13

# GOD'S PROTECTION

*Though I sit in darkness, the Lord will be my light.*
Micah 7:8 HCSB

## THE FOCUS FOR TODAY

God helps those who help themselves, but there are times
when we are quite incapable of helping ourselves.
That's when God stoops down and gathers us in
His arms like a mother lifts a sick child,
and does for us what we cannot do for ourselves.
Ruth Bell Graham

Have you ever faced challenges that seemed too big to handle? Have you ever faced big problems that, despite your best efforts, simply could not be solved? If so, you know how uncomfortable it is to feel helpless in the face of difficult circumstances. Thankfully, even when there's nowhere else to turn, you can turn your thoughts and prayers to God, and He will respond.

God's hand uplifts those who turn their hearts and prayers to Him. Count yourself among that number. When you do, you can live courageously and joyfully, knowing that "this too will pass"—but that God's love for you will not. And you can draw strength from the knowledge that you are a marvelous creation, loved, protected, and uplifted by the ever-present hand of God.

## OPEN YOUR HEART TO HIM

St. Augustine observed, "God loves each of us as if there were only one of us." Do you believe those words? Do you seek to have an intimate, one-on-one relationship with your Heavenly Father, or are you satisfied to keep Him at a "safe" distance?

Sometimes, in the crush of our daily duties, God may seem far away, but He is not. God is everywhere we have ever been and everywhere we will ever go. He is with us night and day; He knows our thoughts and our prayers. And, when we earnestly seek Him, we will find Him because He is here, waiting patiently for us to reach out to Him.

Today, as you carve out quiet moments of thanksgiving and praise for your Heavenly Father, open yourself to His presence and to His love. He is here, waiting. His love is here, always. Accept it—now—and be blessed.

---

### SOMETHING TO REMEMBER

In dealing with difficult situations, view God as your comfort and your strength. Through good times and bad, God is always with you, and you are always protected.

---

## MORE FROM GOD'S WORD ABOUT GOD'S PROTECTION

*Finally, my brethren, be strong in the Lord and in the power of His might. Put on the whole armor of God, that you may be able to stand against the wiles of the devil.*

Ephesians 6:10-11 NKJV

*The Lord your God in your midst, The Mighty One, will save; He will rejoice over you with gladness, He will quiet you with His love, He will rejoice over you with singing.*

Zephaniah 3:17 NKJV

*God is my shield, saving those whose hearts are true and right.*

Psalm 7:10 NLT

*Those who trust the Lord are like Mount Zion, which sits unmoved forever. As the mountains surround Jerusalem, the Lord surrounds his people now and forever.*

Psalm 125:1-2 NCV

*But the Lord will be a refuge for His people.*

Joel 3:16 HCSB

## MORE FROM GOD'S WORD ABOUT GOD'S LOVE

*We know how much God loves us, and we have put our trust in him. God is love, and all who live in love live in God, and God lives in them.*

1 John 4:16 NLT

*As the Father loved Me, I also have loved you; abide in My love.*

John 15:9 NKJV

*For God so loved the world, that he gave his only begotten Son, that whosoever believeth in him should not perish, but have everlasting life.*

John 3:16 KJV

*The unfailing love of the LORD never ends! By his mercies we have been kept from complete destruction.*

Lamentations 3:22 NLT

*His banner over me was love.*

Song of Solomon 2:4 KJV

## MORE POWERFUL IDEAS ABOUT GOD'S PROTECTION

We all go through pain and sorrow, but the presence of God, like a warm, comforting blanket, can shield us and protect us, and allow the deep inner joy to surface, even in the most devastating circumstances.

*Barbara Johnson*

Whatever hallway you're in—no matter how long, how dark, or how scary—God is right there with you.

*Bill Hybels*

Adversity is always unexpected and unwelcomed. It is an intruder and a thief, and yet in the hands of God, adversity becomes the means through which His supernatural power is demonstrated.

*Charles Stanley*

Things can be very difficult for us, but nothing is too hard for Him.

*Charles Stanley*

The only way to learn a strong faith is to endure great trials. I have learned my faith by standing firm amid the most severe of tests.

*George Mueller*

## MORE POWERFUL IDEAS ABOUT GOD'S LOVE

God will never let you sink under your circumstances. He always provides a safety net and His love always encircles.

Barbara Johnson

If we make our troubles an opportunity to learn more of God's love and His power to aid and bless, then they will teach us to have a firmer confidence in His Providence.

Billy Graham

When we hit a tough spot, our tendency is to feel abandoned. In fact, just the opposite is true, for at that moment, we are more than ever the object of God's concern.

Charles Swindoll

When God allows extraordinary trials for His people, He prepares extraordinary comforts for them.

Corrie ten Boom

We cannot protect ourselves from trouble, but we can dance through the puddles of life with a rainbow smile, twirling the only umbrella we need—the umbrella of God's love.

Barbara Johnson

## QUESTIONS TO CONSIDER

Do I believe that God will protect me now and throughout eternity?

_____

_____

Do I trust God's plans even when I cannot understand them?

_____

_____

Am I willing to accept God's unfolding plan for the world—and for my world?

_____

_____

### A PRAYER FOR TODAY

_Lord, sometimes life is difficult. Sometimes, I am worried, weary, or heartbroken. And sometimes, I encounter powerful temptations to disobey Your commandments. But, when I lift my eyes to You, Father, You strengthen me. When I am weak, You lift me up. Today, I will turn to You for strength, for hope, for direction, and for deliverance. Amen_

# Day 14

# In Tough Times, God Teaches and Leads

*Leave inexperience behind, and you will live;*
*pursue the way of understanding.*
Proverbs 9:6 HCSB

## The Focus for Today

Your greatest ministry will likely come out
of your greatest hurt.
Rick Warren

From time to time, all of us encounter circumstances that test our faith. When we encounter life's inevitable tragedies, trials, and disappointments, we may be tempted to blame God or to rebel against Him. But the Bible reminds us that the trials of life can and should be viewed as tools through which we become "mature and complete, lacking nothing."

Have you recently encountered one of life's inevitable tests? If so, remember that God still has lessons that He intends to teach you. So ask yourself this: what lesson is God trying to teach me today?

## WHERE IS GOD LEADING?

Whether we realize it or not, times of adversity can be times of intense personal and spiritual growth. Our difficult days are also times when we can learn and relearn some of life's most important lessons.

The next time you experience a difficult moment, a difficult day, or a difficult year, ask yourself this question: Where is God leading me? In times struggle and sorrow, you can be certain that God is leading you to a place of His choosing. Your duty is to watch, to pray, to listen, and to follow.

SOMETHING TO REMEMBER

Times of change can be times of growth. Elisabeth Elliot reminds us that tough times can lead to a renewal of spirit: "If the leaves had not been let go to fall and wither, if the tree had not consented to be a skeleton for many months, there would be no new life rising, no bud, no flower, no fruit, no seed, no new generation."

## More from God's Word About Spiritual Growth

*For this reason we also, since the day we heard it, do not cease to pray for you, and to ask that you may be filled with the knowledge of His will in all wisdom and spiritual understanding.*

Colossians 1:9 NKJV

*So let us stop going over the basics of Christianity again and again. Let us go on instead and become mature in our understanding.*

Hebrews 6:1 NLT

*Run away from infantile indulgence. Run after mature righteousness—faith, love, peace—joining those who are in honest and serious prayer before God.*

2 Timothy 2:22 MSG

*For You, O God, have tested us; You have refined us as silver is refined. You brought us into the net; You laid affliction on our backs. You have caused men to ride over our heads; we went through fire and through water; but You brought us out to rich fulfillment.*

Psalm 66:10–12 NKJV

## MORE POWERFUL IDEAS ABOUT SPIRITUAL GROWTH

Let's thank God for allowing us to experience troubles that drive us closer to Him.

Shirley Dobson

It is a fact of Christian experience that life is a series of troughs and peaks. In his efforts to get permanent possession of a soul, God relies on the troughs more than the peaks. And, some of his special favorites have gone through longer and deeper troughs than anyone else.

Peter Marshall

Growth in depth and strength and consistency and fruitfulness and ultimately in Christlikeness is only possible when the winds of life are contrary to personal comfort.

Anne Graham Lotz

Comfort and prosperity have never enriched the world as much as adversity has.

Billy Graham

Meditation is as silver; but tribulation is as fine gold.

C. H. Spurgeon

## QUESTIONS TO CONSIDER

Do I believe that God has lessons to teach me?

_____

_____

Do I believe that I still have "room to grow" in my faith?

_____

_____

Do I believe that spiritual growth usually happens day by day, and do I try to keep growing every day?

_____

_____

### A PRAYER FOR TODAY

_Dear Lord, when I open myself to You, I am blessed. Let me accept Your love and Your wisdom, Father. Show me Your way, and deliver me from the painful mistakes that I make when I stray from Your commandments. Let me live according to Your Word, and let me grow in my faith every day that I live. Amen_

# Day 15

# SELF-ESTEEM ACCORDING TO GOD

*For you made us only a little lower than God,*
*and you crowned us with glory and honor.*

Psalm 8:5 NLT

## THE FOCUS FOR TODAY

Being loved by Him whose opinion matters most gives us
the security to risk loving, too—even loving ourselves.

Gloria Gaither

When you encounter tough times, you may lose self-confidence. Or you may become so focused on what other people are thinking—or saying—that you fail to focus on God. To do so is a mistake of major proportions—don't make it. Instead, seek God's guidance as you focus your energies on becoming the best you that you can possibly be. And when it comes to matters of self-esteem and self-image, seek approval not from your peers, but from your Creator.

Millions of words have been written about various ways to improve self-image and increase self-esteem. Yet, maintaining a healthy self-image is, to a surprising extent, a matter of doing three things: 1. Obeying God. 2. Thinking healthy thoughts. 3. Finding a purpose for your life that pleases your Creator and yourself. The following common-sense, Biblically-based tips can help you build the kind of self-image—and the kind of life—that both you and God can be proud of:

1. Do the right thing: If you're misbehaving, how can you possibly hope to feel good about yourself? (See Romans 14:12)

2. Watch what you think: If your inner voice is, in reality, your inner critic, you need to tone down the criticism now. And while you're at it, train yourself to begin thinking thoughts that are more rational, more accepting, and less judgmental. (Philippians 4:8)

3. Spend time with boosters, not critics: Are your friends putting you down? If so, find new friends. (Hebrews 3:13)

4. Don't be a perfectionist: Strive for excellence, but never confuse it with perfection. (Ecclesiastes 11:4, 6)

5. If you're addicted to something unhealthy, stop; if you can't stop, get help: Addictions, of whatever type, create havoc in your life. And disorder. And grief. And low self-esteem. (Exodus 20:3)

6. Find a purpose for your life that is larger than you are: When you're dedicated to something or someone besides yourself, you blossom. (Ephesians 6:7)

7. Don't worry too much about self-esteem: Instead, worry more about living a life that is pleasing to God. Learn to think optimistically. Find a worthy purpose. Find people to love and people to serve. When you do, your self-esteem will, on most days, take care of itself.

---

SOMETHING TO REMEMBER

Don't make the mistake of selling yourself short. No matter the size of your challenges, you can be sure that you and God, working together, can tackle them.

## MORE FROM GOD'S WORD ABOUT YOUR SELF-WORTH

*You're blessed when you're content with just who you are—no more, no less. That's the moment you find yourselves proud owners of everything that can't be bought.*

Matthew 5:5 MSG

*A devout life does bring wealth, but it's the rich simplicity of being yourself before God.*

1 Timothy 6:6 MSG

*You made all the delicate, inner parts of my body and knit me together in my mother's womb. Thank you for making me so wonderfully complex! Your workmanship is marvelous—and how well I know it.*

Psalm 139:13-14 NLT

*My dear children, let's not just talk about love; let's practice real love. This is the only way we'll know we're living truly, living in God's reality. It's also the way to shut down debilitating self-criticism, even when there is something to it. For God is greater than our worried hearts and knows more about us than we do ourselves. And friends, once that's taken care of and we're no longer accusing or condemning ourselves, we're bold and free before God!*

1 John 3:18-21 MSG

## MORE POWERFUL IDEAS ABOUT YOUR SELF-WORTH

As you and I lay up for ourselves living, lasting treasures in heaven, we come to the awesome conclusion that we ourselves are His treasure!

Anne Graham Lotz

The Creator has made us each one of a kind. There is nobody else exactly like us, and there never will be. Each of us is his special creation and is alive for a distinctive purpose.

Luci Swindoll

Comparison is the root of all feelings of inferiority.

James Dobson

When it comes to our position before God, we're perfect. When he sees each of us, he sees one who has been made perfect through the One who is perfect—Jesus Christ.

Max Lucado

Give yourself a gift today: be present with yourself. God is. Enjoy your own personality. God does.

Barbara Johnson

Your self worth is more important than your net worth.

Anonymous

## QUESTIONS TO CONSIDER

Do I pay careful attention to the messages that I'm sending myself about myself?

_____

_____

Am I sometimes my own worst critic, and is the criticism really deserved?

_____

_____

Do I remind myself that God loves me . . . and that I should, too?

_____

_____

## A PRAYER FOR TODAY
_Dear Lord, help me speak courteously to everyone, including myself. And when I make a mistake, help me to forgive myself quickly and thoroughly, just as I forgive others. Amen_

# Day 16

# GUARDING YOUR THOUGHTS

*Finally brothers, whatever is true, whatever is honorable,
whatever is just, whatever is pure, whatever is lovely,
whatever is commendable—if there is any moral excellence
and if there is any praise—dwell on these things.*

Philippians 4:8 HCSB

## THE FOCUS FOR TODAY

Your thoughts are the determining factor as to whose
mold you are conformed to. Control your thoughts
and you control the direction of your life.

Charles Stanley

Are you an optimistic, hopeful, enthusiastic Christian? You should be. After all, as a believer, you have every reason to be optimistic about life here on earth and life eternal. As English clergyman William Ralph Inge observed, "No Christian should be a pessimist, for Christianity is a system of radical optimism." Inge's words are most certainly true, but sometimes, you may find yourself pulled down by tough times. If you find yourself discouraged, exhausted, or both, then it's time to ask yourself this question: what's bothering you, and why?

If you're worried by the inevitable challenges of everyday living, God wants to have a little talk with you. After all, the ultimate battle has already been won on the cross at Calvary. And if your life has been transformed by Christ's sacrifice, then you, as a recipient of God's grace, have every reason to live courageously.

Are you willing to trust God's plans for your life, in good times and hard times? Hopefully, you will trust Him completely. Proverbs 3:5-6 makes it clear: "Trust in the Lord with all your heart, and lean not on your own understanding; in all your ways acknowledge Him, and He shall direct your paths" (NKJV).

A. W. Tozer noted, "Attitude is all-important. Let the soul take a quiet attitude of faith and love toward God, and from there on, the responsibility is God's. He will make good on His commitments." These words should serve as a reminder that even when the challenges of the day seem daunting, God remains steadfast. And, so should you.

So make this promise to yourself and keep it—vow to be a hope-filled Christian. Think optimistically about your life, your profession, your family, your future, and your purpose for living. Trust your hopes, not your fears. Take time to celebrate God's glorious creation. And then, when you've filled your heart with hope and gladness, share your optimism with others. They'll be better for it, and so will you.

---

### SOMETHING TO REMEMBER

Be a realistic optimist. Your attitude toward the future will help create your future. So think realistically about yourself and your situation while making a conscious effort to focus on hopes, not fears. When you do, you'll put the self-fulfilling prophecy to work for you.

## MORE FROM GOD'S WORD ABOUT YOUR THOUGHTS

*So prepare your minds for service and have self-control.*

1 Peter 1:13 NCV

*Come near to God, and God will come near to you. You sinners, clean sin out of your lives. You who are trying to follow God and the world at the same time, make your thinking pure.*

James 4:8 NCV

*Those who are pure in their thinking are happy, because they will be with God.*

Matthew 5:8 NCV

*Do not conform any longer to the pattern of this world, but be transformed by the renewing of your mind. Then you will be able to test and approve what God's will is—his good, pleasing and perfect will.*

Romans 12:2 NIV

*Dear friend, guard Clear Thinking and Common Sense with your life; don't for a minute lose sight of them. They'll keep your soul alive and well, they'll keep you fit and attractive.*

Proverbs 3:21-22 MSG

## MORE FROM GOD'S WORD ABOUT HOPE

*The lines of purpose in your lives never grow slack, tightly tied as they are to your future in heaven, kept taut by hope.*

Colossians 1:5 MSG

*Let us hold fast the confession of our hope without wavering, for He who promised is faithful.*

Hebrews 10:23 NASB

*Now faith is the substance of things hoped for, the evidence of things not seen.*

Hebrews 11:1 KJV

*This hope we have as an anchor of the soul, a hope both sure and steadfast.*

Hebrews 6:19 NASB

*Full of hope, you'll relax, confident again; you'll look around, sit back, and take it easy.*

Job 11:18 MSG

## MORE POWERFUL IDEAS ABOUT YOUR THOUGHTS

The things we think are the things that feed our souls. If we think on pure and lovely things, we shall grow pure and lovely like them; and the converse is equally true.

Hannah Whitall Smith

Every major spiritual battle is in the mind.

Charles Stanley

It is the thoughts and intents of the heart that shape a person's life.

John Eldredge

People who do not develop and practice good thinking often find themselves at the mercy of their circumstances.

John Maxwell

I became aware of one very important concept I had missed before: my attitude—not my circumstances—was what was making me unhappy.

Vonette Bright

Attitude is the mind's paintbrush; it can color any situation.

Barbara Johnson

## MORE POWERFUL IDEAS ABOUT HOPE

Never yield to gloomy anticipation. Place your hope and confidence in God. He has no record of failure.

Mrs. Charles E. Cowman

I wish I could make it all new again; I can't. But God can. "He restores my soul," wrote the shepherd. God doesn't reform; he restores. He doesn't camouflage the old; he restores the new. The Master Builder will pull out the original plan and restore it. He will restore the vigor, he will restore the energy. He will restore the hope. He will restore the soul.

Max Lucado

The best we can hope for in this life is a knothole peek at the shining realities ahead. Yet a glimpse is enough. It's enough to convince our hearts that whatever sufferings and sorrows currently assail us aren't worthy of comparison to that which waits over the horizon.

Joni Eareckson Tada

Faith looks back and draws courage; hope looks ahead and keeps desire alive.

John Eldredge

## QUESTIONS TO CONSIDER

Do I understand the importance of directing my thoughts in a proper direction?

_____

_____

Do I believe that emotions are contagious, and do I try to associate with people who are upbeat, optimistic, and encouraging?

_____

_____

Do I understand that when I dwell on positive thoughts, I feel better about myself and my circumstances?

_____

_____

### A PRAYER FOR TODAY
_Lord, I will focus on Your love, Your power, Your
promises, and Your Son. When I am weak, I will turn
to You for strength; when I am troubled, I will turn to
You for patience and perspective. Help me guard my
thoughts, Lord, so that I may honor You
this day and forever. Amen_

# Day 17

# THE THINGS YOU CANNOT CHANGE

*I have learned to be content in whatever circumstances I am.*
Philippians 4:11 HCSB

## THE FOCUS FOR TODAY

People, places, and things were never meant to give us life. God alone is the author of a fulfilling life.
Gary Smalley & John Trent

The words of Matthew 4:4 remind us that, "Man shall not live by bread alone but by every word that proceedeth out of the mouth of God" (KJV). As believers, we must study the Bible and meditate upon its meaning for our lives. Otherwise, we deprive ourselves of a priceless gift from our Creator.

God's Word is unlike any other book. The Bible is a roadmap for life here on earth and for life eternal. As Christians, we are called upon to study God's Holy Word, to follow its commandments, and to share its Good News with the world.

Jonathan Edwards advised, "Be assiduous in reading the Holy Scriptures. This is the fountain whence all knowledge in divinity must be derived. Therefore let not this treasure lie by you neglected." God's Holy Word is, indeed, a priceless, one-of-a-kind treasure, and a passing acquaintance with the Good Book is insufficient for Christians who seek to obey God's Word and to understand His will. After all, man does not live by bread alone . . .

## GOD'S WORD REDUCES STRESS

If you're experiencing stress, God's Word can help relieve it. And if you'd like to experience God's peace, Bible study can help provide it.

Warren Wiersbe observed, "When the child of God looks into the Word of God, he sees the Son of God. And, he is transformed by the Spirit of God to share in the glory of God." God's Holy Word is, indeed, a life-changing, stress-reducing, one-of-a-kind treasure. And it's up to you—and only you—to use it that way.

---

### SOMETHING TO REMEMBER

If you have a choice to make, the Bible can help you make it. If you've got questions, the Bible has answers. So take a Bible with you wherever you go. You never know when you may need a midday spiritual pick-me-up.

---

## MORE FROM GOD'S WORD ABOUT GOD'S WORD

*This is my comfort in my affliction, for Your word has given me life.*

Psalm 119:50 NKJV

*Let the Word of Christ—the Message—have the run of the house. Give it plenty of room in your lives. Instruct and direct one another using good common sense. And sing, sing your hearts out to God! Let every detail in your lives—words, actions, whatever—be done in the name of the Master, Jesus, thanking God the Father every step of the way.*

Colossians 3:16-17 MSG

*For the word of God is living and active. Sharper than any double-edged sword, it penetrates even to dividing soul and spirit, joints and marrow; it judges the thoughts and attitudes of the heart.*

Hebrews 4:12 NIV

*For as the rain comes down, and the snow from heaven, and do not return there, but water the earth, and make it bring forth and bud, that it may give seed to the sower and bread to the eater, so shall My word be that goes forth from My mouth; it shall not return to Me void, but it shall accomplish what I please, and it shall prosper in the thing for which I sent it.*

Isaiah 55:10-11 NKJV

## MORE POWERFUL IDEAS ABOUT GOD'S WORD

God has given us all sorts of counsel and direction in his written Word; thank God, we have it written down in black and white.

John Eldredge

The Bible is God's Word, given to us by God Himself so we can know Him and His will for our lives.

Billy Graham

Nobody ever outgrows Scripture; the book widens and deepens with our years.

C. H. Spurgeon

Prayer and the Word are inseparably linked together. Power in the use of either depends on the presence of the other.

Andrew Murray

If you want to know whether you're thinking correctly, check it out in the Word.

Charles Stanley

*But the word of the Lord
endures forever.
And this is the word
that was preached
as the gospel to you.*

—

1 Peter 1:25 HCSB

## MORE POWERFUL IDEAS ABOUT BIBLE STUDY

Only through routine, regular exposure to God's Word can you and I draw out the nutrition needed to grow a heart of faith.

*Elizabeth George*

I believe the reason so many are failing today is that they have not disciplined themselves to read God's Word consistently, day in and day out, and to apply it to every situation in life.

*Kay Arthur*

Weave the unveiling fabric of God's Word through your heart and mind. It will hold strong, even if the rest of life unravels.

*Gigi Graham Tchividjian*

If we neglect the Bible, we cannot expect to benefit from the wisdom and direction that result from knowing God's Word.

*Vonette Bright*

Help me, Lord, to be a student of Your Word, that I might be a better servant in Your world.

*Jim Gallery*

## QUESTIONS TO CONSIDER

Do I make it a priority to read the Bible every day?

_____

_____

Do I consider regular Bible study to be an important source of wisdom?

_____

_____

Do I have a systematic plan for studying God's Word?

_____

_____

### A PRAYER FOR TODAY

*Heavenly Father, Your Word is a light unto the world;*
*I will study it, and trust it, and share it. In all that*
*I do, help me be a worthy witness for You as*
*I share the Good News of Your perfect Son*
*and Your perfect Word. Amen*

# Day 18

# DON'T GIVE UP!

*No matter how many times you trip them up, God-loyal people don't stay down long; Soon they're up on their feet, while the wicked end up flat on their faces.*

Proverbs 24:16 MSG

## THE FOCUS FOR TODAY

We don't give up. We look up. We trust. We believe. And our optimism is not hollow. Christ has proven worthy. He has shown that he never fails. That's what makes God, God.

Max Lucado

The old saying is as true today as it was when it was first spoken: "Life is a marathon, not a sprint." That's why wise travelers (like you) select a traveling companion who never tires and never falters. That partner, of course, is your Heavenly Father.

Perhaps you are in a hurry for God to help you resolve your difficulties. Perhaps you're anxious to earn the rewards that you feel you've already earned from life. Perhaps you're drumming your fingers, impatiently waiting for God to act. If so, be forewarned: God operates on His own timetable, not yours. Sometimes, God may answer your prayers with silence, and when He does, you must patiently persevere. In times of trouble, you must remain steadfast and trust in the merciful goodness of your Heavenly Father. Whatever your problem, He can handle it. Your job is to keep persevering until He does.

## HE OVERCOMES THE WORLD

Today he's a respected pastor in Memphis, Tennessee. But in the 1970's, he was just about as far from the church as he could get. As one of the best-selling recording artists in the world, Al Green lived life in the fast lane, and he didn't spend much time thinking or talking about God. But all that changed in 1977 when Green faced a personal tragedy that caused him to reassess his life and turn it over to God.

Reverend Al's advice is straightforward. He says, "If you just hang in there with God, everything's gonna be alright."

---

### SOMETHING TO REMEMBER

Are you being tested? Call upon God. The next time you find your courage tested to the limit, remember that God is as near as your next breath, and remember that He offers strength and comfort to His children. He is your shield, your protector, and your deliverer. Call upon Him in your hour of need and then be comforted. Whatever your challenge, whatever your trouble, God can give you the strength to persevere, and that's exactly what you should ask Him to do.

## MORE FROM GOD'S WORD ABOUT PERSEVERANCE

*Let us not become weary in doing good, for at the proper time we will reap a harvest if we do not give up.*

Galatians 6:9 NIV

*For you have need of endurance, so that when you have done the will of God, you may receive what was promised.*

Hebrews 10:36 NASB

*Thanks be to God! He gives us the victory through our Lord Jesus Christ. Therefore, my dear brothers, stand firm. Let nothing move you. Always give yourselves fully to the work of the Lord, because you know that your labor in the Lord is not in vain.*

1 Corinthians 15:57-58 NIV

*Be diligent that ye may be found of him in peace, without spot, and blameless.*

2 Peter 3:14 KJV

*It is better to finish something than to start it. It is better to be patient than to be proud.*

Ecclesiastes 7:8 NCV

## MORE POWERFUL IDEAS ABOUT PERSEVERANCE

The sermon of your life in tough times ministers to people more powerfully than the most eloquent speaker.

Bill Bright

Failure is one of life's most powerful teachers. How we handle our failures determines whether we're going to simply "get by" in life or "press on."

Beth Moore

As we wait on God, He helps us use the winds of adversity to soar above our problems. As the Bible says, "Those who wait on the LORD . . . shall mount up with wings like eagles."

Billy Graham

Are you a Christian? If you are, how can you be hopeless? Are you so depressed by the greatness of your problems that you have given up all hope? Instead of giving up, would you patiently endure? Would you focus on Christ until you are so preoccupied with him alone that you fall prostrate before him?

Anne Graham Lotz

## QUESTIONS TO CONSIDER

Do I have a healthy respect for the power of perseverance?

_____

_____

When I am discouraged, do I ask God to give me strength?

_____

_____

Do I associate with people who encourage me to be courageous, optimistic, energetic, and persistent?

_____

_____

### A PRAYER FOR TODAY

*Lord, when life is difficult, I am tempted to abandon hope in the future. But You are my God, and I can draw strength from You. Let me trust You, Father, in good times and in bad times. Let me persevere—even if my soul is troubled—and let me follow Your Son, Jesus Christ, this day and forever. Amen*

# Day 19

# LIVE COURAGEOUSLY

*They do not fear bad news; they confidently trust the Lord*
*to care for them. They are confident and fearless*
*and can face their foes triumphantly.*

Psalm 112:7-8 NLT

## THE FOCUS FOR TODAY

Faith not only can help you through a crisis,
it can help you to approach life after the hard times with
a whole new perspective. It can help you adopt
an outlook of hope and courage through
faith to face reality.

John Maxwell

Every person's life is a tapestry of events: some wonderful, some not-so-wonderful, and some downright disastrous. When we visit the mountaintops of life, praising God isn't hard—in fact, it's easy. In our moments of triumph, we can bow our heads and thank God for our victories. But when we fail to reach the mountaintops, when we endure the inevitable losses that are a part of every person's life, we find it much tougher to give God the praise He deserves. Yet wherever we find ourselves, whether on the mountaintops of life or in life's darkest valleys, we must still offer thanks to God, giving thanks in all circumstances.

The next time you find yourself worried about the challenges of today or the uncertainties of tomorrow, ask yourself this question: are you really ready to place your concerns and your life in God's all-powerful, all-knowing, all-loving hands? If the answer to that question is yes—as it should be—then you can draw courage today from the source of strength that never fails: your Father in heaven.

God is not a distant being. He is not absent from our world, nor is He absent from your world. God is not "out there"; He is "right here," continuously reshaping His universe, and continuously reshaping the lives of those who dwell in it.

God is with you always, listening to your thoughts and prayers, watching over your every move. If the demands of everyday life weigh down upon you, you may be tempted to ignore God's presence or—worse yet—to lose faith in His promises. But, when you quiet yourself and acknowledge His presence, God will touch your heart and restore your courage.

At this very moment—as you're fulfilling your obligations and overcoming tough times—God is seeking to work in you and through you. He's asking you to live abundantly and courageously . . . and He's ready to help. So why not let Him do it . . . starting now?

---

SOMETHING TO REMEMBER

With God as your partner, you have nothing to fear. Why? Because you and God, working together, can handle absolutely anything that comes your way. So the next time you'd like an extra measure of courage, recommit yourself to a true one-on-one relationship with your Creator. When you sincerely turn to Him, He will never fail you.

## MORE FROM GOD'S WORD ABOUT COURAGE

*Be strong and courageous, and do the work. Don't be afraid or discouraged by the size of the task, for the LORD God, my God, is with you. He will not fail you or forsake you.*

1 Chronicles 28:20 NLT

*Therefore, being always of good courage . . . we walk by faith, not by sight.*

2 Corinthians 5:6-7 NASB

*God doesn't want us to be shy with his gifts, but bold and loving and sensible.*

2 Timothy 1:7 MSG

*The LORD himself goes before you and will be with you; he will never leave you nor forsake you. Do not be afraid; do not be discouraged.*

Deuteronomy 31:8 NIV

*But Moses said to the people, "Do not fear! Stand by and see the salvation of the LORD."*

Exodus 14:13 NASB

## MORE FROM GOD'S WORD ABOUT STRENGTH

*And He said to me, "My grace is sufficient for you, for My strength is made perfect in weakness."*

2 Corinthians 12:9 NKJV

*He gives strength to the weary and strengthens the powerless.*

Isaiah 40:29 HCSB

*Finally, be strengthened by the Lord and by His vast strength.*

Ephesians 6:10 HCSB

*You, therefore, my child, be strong in the grace that is in Christ Jesus.*

2 Timothy 2:1 HCSB

*The Lord is my strength and my song; He has become my salvation.*

Exodus 15:2 HCSB

## MORE POWERFUL IDEAS ABOUT COURAGE

Seeing that a Pilot steers the ship in which we sail, who will never allow us to perish even in the midst of shipwrecks, there is no reason why our minds should be overwhelmed with fear and overcome with weariness.

John Calvin

Like dynamite, God's power is only latent power until it is released. You can release God's dynamite power into people's lives and into the world through faith, through words, and through prayer.

Bill Bright

Faith is stronger than fear.

John Maxwell

Do not let Satan deceive you into being afraid of God's plans for your life.

R. A. Torrey

Jesus Christ can make the weakest man into a divine dreadnought, fearing nothing.

Oswald Chambers

Perhaps I am stronger than I think.

Thomas Merton

## MORE POWERFUL IDEAS ABOUT STRENGTH

God does not dispense strength and encouragement like a druggist fills your prescription. The Lord doesn't promise to give us something to take so we can handle our weary moments. He promises us Himself. That is all. And that is enough.

Charles Swindoll

We are not called to be burden-bearers, but cross-bearers and light-bearers. We must cast our burdens on the Lord.

Corrie ten Boom

God does not promise to protect us from trials, but to protect us in trials. The dangers of life may hurt us but they can never harm us.

Warren Wiersbe

No matter how heavy the burden, daily strength is given, so I expect we need not give ourselves any concern as to what the outcome will be. We must simply go forward.

Annie Armstrong

When we spend time with Christ, He supplies us with strength and encourages us in the pursuit of His ways.

Elizabeth George

## QUESTIONS TO CONSIDER

Do I consider God to be my partner in every aspect of my life?

_____

_____

Do I trust God to handle the problems that are simply too big for me to solve?

_____

_____

Am I really willing to place my future in God's hands?

_____

_____

## A PRAYER FOR TODAY

*Lord, sometimes I face challenges that leave me breathless. When I am fearful, let me lean upon You. Keep me ever mindful, Lord, that You are my God, my strength, and my shield. With You by my side, I have nothing to fear. And, with Your Son Jesus as my Savior, I have received the priceless gift of eternal life. Help me to be a grateful and courageous servant this day and every day. Amen*

# Day 20

# YOU'RE NEVER ALONE

*The Lord is the One who will go before you.*
*He will be with you; He will not leave you or forsake you.*
*Do not be afraid or discouraged.*
Deuteronomy 31:8 HCSB

## THE FOCUS FOR TODAY

God is in the midst of whatever has happened,
is happening, and will happen.
Charles Swindoll

If God is everywhere, why does He sometimes seem so far away? The answer to that question, of course, has nothing to do with God and everything to do with us.

When we begin each day on our knees, in praise and worship to Him, God often seems very near indeed. But, if we ignore God's presence or—worse yet—rebel against it altogether, the world in which we live becomes a spiritual wasteland.

Are you tired, discouraged or fearful? Be comforted because God is with you. Are you confused? Listen to the quiet voice of your Heavenly Father. Are you bitter? Talk with God and seek His guidance. Are you celebrating a great victory? Thank God and praise Him. He is the Giver of all things good.

In whatever condition you find yourself, wherever you are, whether you are happy or sad, victorious or vanquished, troubled or triumphant, celebrate God's presence.

## SPENDING QUIET MOMENTS WITH GOD

We live in a fast-paced world. The demands of everyday life can seem overwhelming at times, but when we slow ourselves down and seek the presence of a loving God, we invite His peace into our hearts.

Do you set aside quiet moments each day to offer praise to your Creator? You should. During these moments of stillness, you will often sense the infinite love and power of our Lord.

The familiar words of Psalm 46:10 remind us to "Be still, and know that I am God." When we do so, we encounter the awesome presence of our loving Heavenly Father, and we are comforted in the knowledge that God is not just near. He is here.

---

### SOMETHING TO REMEMBER

Having trouble hearing God? If so, slow yourself down, tune out the distractions, and listen carefully. God has important things to say; your task is to be still and listen.

---

## MORE FROM GOD'S WORD ABOUT GOD'S PRESENCE

*Come near to God, and God will come near to you. You sinners, clean sin out of your lives. You who are trying to follow God and the world at the same time, make your thinking pure.*

James 4:8 NCV

*No, I will not abandon you as orphans—I will come to you.*

John 14:18 NLT

*Again, this is God's command: to believe in his personally named Son, Jesus Christ. He told us to love each other, in line with the original command. As we keep his commands, we live deeply and surely in him, and he lives in us. And this is how we experience his deep and abiding presence in us: by the Spirit he gave us.*

1 John 3:23-24 MSG

*For the eyes of the Lord range throughout the earth to strengthen those whose hearts are fully committed to him.*

2 Chronicles 16:9 NIV

*God did this so that men would seek him and perhaps reach out for him and find him, though he is not far from each one of us.*

Acts 17:27 NIV

# More Powerful Ideas About God's Presence

God's silence is in no way indicative of His activity or involvement in our lives. He may be silent, but He is not still.

Charles Swindoll

We should learn to live in the presence of the living God. He should be a well for us: delightful, comforting, unfailing, springing up to eternal life (John 4:14). When we rely on other people, their water supplies ultimately dry up. But, the well of the Creator never fails to nourish us.

C. H. Spurgeon

Certainly, God is with us in times of distress, and that is a comforting truth. But listen: Jesus wants to be part of every experience and every moment of our lives.

Billy Graham

Get yourself into the presence of the loving Father. Just place yourself before Him, and look up into, His face; think of His love, His wonderful, tender, pitying love.

Andrew Murray

## MORE POWERFUL IDEAS ABOUT GOD'S PRESENCE

We all go through pain and sorrow, but the presence of God, like a warm, comforting blanket, can shield us and protect us, and allow the deep inner joy to surface, even in the most devastating circumstances.

*Barbara Johnson*

Often, in the midst of great problems, we stop short of the real blessing God has for us, which is a fresh vision of who He is.

*Anne Graham Lotz*

God walks with us. He scoops us up in His arms or simply sits with us in silent strength until we cannot avoid the awesome recognition that yes, even now, He is here.

*Gloria Gaither*

The Lord is the one who travels every mile of the wilderness way as our leader, cheering us, supporting and supplying and fortifying us.

*Elisabeth Elliot*

God whispers to us
in our pleasures,
speaks in our conscience,
but shouts in our pain.

—

C. S. Lewis

## QUESTIONS TO CONSIDER

Do I believe that God seeks a close and intimate relationship with me?

_____

_____

Do I understand that whenever I feel distant from God, that distance is my own doing, not His?

_____

_____

Am I willing to quiet myself long enough to sense God's presence and His love?

_____

_____

## A PRAYER FOR TODAY

_Heavenly Father, even when it seems to me that You
are far away, You never leave my side.
Today and every day, I will strive to feel Your presence,
and I will strive to sense Your love for me. Amen_

# Day 21

# WORSHIP HIM
# EVERY DAY

*God is Spirit, and those who worship Him
must worship in spirit and truth.*
John 4:24 HCSB

## THE FOCUS FOR TODAY

When your grief presses you to the very dust,
worship there.
C. H. Spurgeon

D o you take time each day to worship your Father in heaven, or do you wait until Sunday morning to praise Him for His blessings? The answer to this question will, in large part, determine the quality and direction of your spiritual life.

When we worship God every day of our lives, we are blessed. When we fail to worship God, for whatever reason, we forfeit the spiritual gifts that He intends for us.

Every day provides opportunities to put God where He belongs: at the center of our lives. When we do so, we worship Him not only with our words, but also with our deeds, and that's as it should be. For believers, God comes first. Always first.

## ALWAYS GIVE THANKS

The words of 1 Thessalonians 5:18 remind us to give thanks in every circumstance of life. But sometimes, when our hearts are troubled and our lives seem to be spinning out of control, we don't feel much like thanking the Creator (or anybody else for that matter). Yet God's Word is clear: In all circumstances, our Father offers us His love, His strength, and His grace. And, in all circumstances, we must thank Him.

Have you thanked God today for blessings that are too numerous to count? Have you offered Him your heartfelt prayers and your wholehearted praise? If not, it's time to slow down and offer a prayer of thanksgiving to the One who has given you life on earth and life eternal.

If you are a thoughtful Christian, you will be a thankful Christian. No matter your circumstances, you owe God so much more than you can ever repay, and you owe Him your heartfelt thanks. So thank Him . . . and keep thanking Him, today, tomorrow and forever.

## SOMETHING TO REMEMBER

Worship reminds you of an important truth: God is big enough to handle your problems. But that's not all: When you worship God with a sincere heart, He will guide your steps and bless your life.

## MORE FROM GOD'S WORD ABOUT WORSHIP

*Then saith Jesus unto him, Get thee hence, Satan: for it is written, Thou shalt worship the Lord thy God, and him only shalt thou serve.*

Matthew 4:10 KJV

*Blessed are they which do hunger and thirst after righteousness: for they shall be filled.*

Matthew 5:6 KJV

*Worship the Lord with gladness. Come before him, singing with joy. Acknowledge that the Lord is God! He made us, and we are his. We are his people, the sheep of his pasture.*

Psalm 100:2-3 NLT

*Happy are those who hear the joyful call to worship, for they will walk in the light of your presence, Lord.*

Psalm 89:15 NLT

*God lifted him high and honored him far beyond anyone or anything, ever, so that all created beings in heaven and earth, even those long ago dead and buried, will bow in worship before this Jesus Christ, and call out in praise that he is the Master of all, to the glorious honor of God the Father.*

Philippians 2:9-11 MSG

## MORE FROM GOD'S WORD ABOUT THANKSGIVING

*In everything give thanks; for this is the will of God in Christ Jesus for you.*

1 Thessalonians 5:18 NKJV

*Our prayers for you are always spilling over into thanksgivings. We can't quit thanking God our Father and Jesus our Messiah for you!*

Colossians 1:3 MSG

*My counsel for you is simple and straightforward: Just go ahead with what you've been given. You received Christ Jesus, the Master; now live him. You're deeply rooted in him. You're well constructed upon him. You know your way around the faith. Now do what you've been taught. School's out; quit studying the subject and start living it! And let your living spill over into thanksgiving.*

Colossians 2:6-7 MSG

*Finally, brethren, whatsoever things are true, whatsoever things are honest, whatsoever things are just, whatsoever things are pure, whatsoever things are lovely, whatsoever things are of good report; if there be any virtue, and if there be any praise, think on these things.*

Philippians 4:8 KJV

## MORE POWERFUL IDEAS ABOUT WORSHIP

I am of the opinion that we should not be concerned about working for God until we have learned the meaning and delight of worshipping Him.

A. W. Tozer

To worship Him in truth means to worship Him honestly, without hypocrisy, standing open and transparent before Him.

Anne Graham Lotz

Each time, before you intercede, be quiet first and worship God in His glory. Think of what He can do and how He delights to hear the prayers of His redeemed people. Think of your place and privilege in Christ, and expect great things!

Andrew Murray

Worship is spiritual. Our worship must be more than just outward expression, it must also take place in our spirits.

Franklin Graham

Inside the human heart is an undeniable, spiritual instinct to commune with its Creator.

Jim Cymbala

## MORE POWERFUL IDEAS ABOUT THANKSGIVING

Thanksgiving or complaining—these words express two contrastive attitudes of the souls of God's children in regard to His dealings with them. The soul that gives thanks can find comfort in everything; the soul that complains can find comfort in nothing.

Hannah Whitall Smith

We ought to give thanks for all fortune: if it is "good," because it is good, if "bad because it works in us patience, humility and the contempt of this world and the hope of our eternal country.

C. S. Lewis

It is always possible to be thankful for what is given rather than to complain about what is not given. One or the other becomes a habit of life.

Elisabeth Elliot

Words fail to express my love for this holy Book, my gratitude for its author, for His love and goodness. How shall I thank him for it?

Lottie Moon

It is only with gratitude that life becomes rich.

Dietrich Bonhoeffer

## QUESTIONS TO CONSIDER

Do I believe that it is important to worship God every day of the week, not just on Sundays?

_____

_____

Do I feel that it is important to worship regularly with a community of believers?

_____

_____

Do I have a quiet place where I can go, a place where God seems especially close?

_____

_____

### A PRAYER FOR TODAY

_Heavenly Father, let today and every day be a time of worship. Let me worship You, not only with words and deeds, but also with my heart. In the quiet moments of the day, let me praise You and thank You for creating me, loving me, guiding me, and saving me. Amen_

# Day 22

# CONSIDER THE POSSIBILITIES

*For nothing will be impossible with God.*
Luke 1:37 HCSB

## THE FOCUS FOR TODAY

Man's adversity is God's opportunity.

Matthew Henry

Are you afraid to ask God to do big things—or to make big changes—in your life? Is your faith threadbare and worn? If so, it's time to abandon your doubts and reclaim your faith in God's promises.

Ours is a God of infinite possibilities. But sometimes, because of limited faith and limited understanding, we wrongly assume that God cannot or will not intervene in the affairs of mankind. Such assumptions are simply wrong.

God's Holy Word makes it clear: absolutely nothing is impossible for the Lord. And since the Bible means what it says, you can be comforted in the knowledge that the Creator of the universe can do miraculous things in your own life and in the lives of your loved ones. Your challenge, as a believer, is to take God at His word, and to expect the miraculous.

## OPPORTUNITIES EVERYWHERE

As you look at the landscape of your life, do you see opportunities, possibilities, and blessings, or do you focus, instead, upon the more negative scenery? Do you spend more time counting your blessings or your misfortunes? If you've acquired the unfortunate habit of focusing too intently upon the negative aspects of life, then your spiritual vision is in need of correction.

Whether you realize it or not, opportunities are whirling around you like stars crossing the night sky: beautiful to observe, but too numerous to count. Yet you may be too concerned with the challenges of everyday living to notice those opportunities. That's why you should slow down occasionally, catch your breath, and focus your thoughts on two things: the talents God has given you and the opportunities that He has placed before you. God is leading you in the direction of those opportunities. Your task is to watch carefully, to pray fervently, and to act accordingly.

---

### SOMETHING TO REMEMBER

Focus on possibilities, not roadblocks. The road of life contains a number of potholes and stumbling blocks. Of course you will encounter them from time to time, and so will your family members. But, don't invest large quantities of your life focusing on past misfortunes. On the road of life, regret is a dead end.

## MORE FROM GOD'S WORD ABOUT POSSIBILITIES

*No eye has seen, no ear has heard, no mind has conceived what God has prepared for those who love him.*

1 Corinthians 2:9 NIV

*Make the most of every opportunity.*

Colossians 4:5 NIV

*Let us not lose heart in doing good, for in due time we shall reap if we do not grow weary. So then, while we have opportunity, let us do good to all men, and especially to those who are of the household of the faith.*

Galatians 6:9-10 NASB

*Dear brothers and sisters, whenever trouble comes your way, let it be an opportunity for joy. For when your faith is tested, your endurance has a chance to grow. So let it grow, for when your endurance is fully developed, you will be strong in character and ready for anything.*

James 1:2-4 NLT

*Remember ye not the former things, neither consider the things of old. Behold, I will do a new thing . . . .*

Isaiah 43:18-19 KJV

## MORE POWERFUL IDEAS ABOUT POSSIBILITIES

Often God shuts a door in our face so that he can open the door through which he wants us to go.

Catherine Marshall

Do we not continually pass by blessings innumerable without notice, and instead fix our eyes on what we feel to be our trials and our losses? And, do we not think and talk about our trials until our whole horizon is filled with them, and we almost begin to think we have no blessings at all?

Hannah Whitall Smith

Allow your dreams a place in your prayers and plans. God-given dreams can help you move into the future He is preparing for you.

Barbara Johnson

When God is involved, anything can happen. Be open and stay that way. God has a beautiful way of bringing good vibrations out of broken chords.

Charles Swindoll

God specializes in taking tragedy and turning it into triumph. The greater the tragedy, the greater the potential for triumph.

Charles Stanley

## QUESTIONS TO CONSIDER

Do I place my hopes in God?

_____

_____

Do I prayerfully seek to understand God's plans for my life?

_____

_____

Do I place limitations on myself, and do I place limitations on God's power to use me for His purposes?

_____

_____

### A PRAYER FOR TODAY

_Dear Lord, give me the courage to dream and the faithfulness to trust in Your perfect plan for my life. When I am worried, give me strength for today and hope for tomorrow. Today, Father, I will trust You and honor You with my thoughts, with my prayers, with my actions, and with my dreams. Amen_

# Day 23

# DEFEATING PROCRASTINATION

*If you wait for perfect conditions,*
*you will never get anything done.*
Ecclesiastes 11:4 NLT

## THE FOCUS FOR TODAY

Not now becomes never.
Martin Luther

When tough times arrive, it's easy (and tempting) to avoid those hard-to-do tasks that you would prefer to avoid altogether. But the habit of procrastination takes a double toll: First, important work goes unfinished, and second, valuable energy is wasted in the process of putting off the things that remain undone.

God has created a world that punishes procrastinators and rewards men and women who "do it now." In other words, life doesn't procrastinate. Neither should you. So if you've been putting things off instead of getting things done, here are some things you can do:

1. Have a clear understanding of your short- and long-term goals, and set your priorities in accordance with those goals.

2. When faced with distasteful tasks, do them immediately, preferably first thing in the morning (even if the unpleasantness is a low-priority activity, go ahead and get it out of the way if it can be completed quickly). Dispatching distasteful tasks sooner rather than later will improve the quality of your day and prevent you from wasting untold amounts of energy in the process of fighting against yourself.

3. Avoid the trap of perfectionism. Be willing to do your best, and be satisfied with the results.

4. If you don't already own one, purchase a daily or weekly planning system that fits your needs. If used properly, a planning calendar is worth many times what you pay for it.

5. Start each work day with a clearly written "to-do" list, ranked according to importance. At lunch time, take a moment to collect your thoughts, reexamine your list, and refocus your efforts on the most important things you wish to accomplish during the remainder of the day.

---

### SOMETHING TO REMEMBER

The habit of procrastination is often rooted in the fear of failure, the fear of discomfort, or the fear of embarrassment. Your challenge is to confront these fears and defeat them.

---

## MORE FROM GOD'S WORD ABOUT PROCRASTINATION

*If you do nothing in a difficult time, your strength is limited.*

Proverbs 24:10 HCSB

*If you are too lazy to plow in the right season, you will have no food at the harvest.*

Proverbs 20:4 NLT

*When you make a vow to God, do not delay in fulfilling it. He has no pleasure in fools; fulfill your vow.*

Ecclesiastes 5:4 NIV

*We can't afford to waste a minute, must not squander these precious daylight hours in frivolity and indulgence, in sleeping around and dissipation, in bickering and grabbing everything in sight. Get out of bed and get dressed! Don't loiter and linger, waiting until the very last minute. Dress yourselves in Christ, and be up and about!*

Romans 13:13-14 MSG

*Whatever you do, do it enthusiastically, as something done for the Lord and not for men.*

Colossians 3:23 HCSB

## MORE POWERFUL IDEAS ABOUT PROCRASTINATION

I've found that the worst thing I can do when it comes to any kind of potential pressure situation is to put off dealing with it.

John Maxwell

Do the unpleasant work first and enjoy the rest of the day.

Marie T. Freeman

I cannot fix what I will not face.

Jim Gallery

Do not build up obstacles in your imagination. Difficulties must be studied and dealt with, but they must not be magnified by fear.

Norman Vincent Peale

Never confuse activity with productivity.

Rick Warren

Do noble things, do not dream them all day long.

Charles Kingsley

### QUESTIONS TO CONSIDER

When something needs to be done, do I see the wisdom in doing it sooner rather than later?

_____

_____

Is the fear of failure holding me back?

_____

_____

When faced with an unpleasant job, do I act promptly, or do I increase my misery by procrastinating?

_____

_____

### A PRAYER FOR TODAY
_Dear Lord, when I am confronted with things
that need to be done, give me the courage
and the wisdom to do them now, not later. Amen_

# Day 24

# TOO FOCUSED ON POSSESSIONS?

*Don't collect for yourselves treasures on earth, where moth
and rust destroy and where thieves break in and steal.
But collect for yourselves treasures in heaven, where neither
moth nor rust destroys, and where thieves don't break in and
steal. For where your treasure is, there your heart will be also.*

Matthew 6:19-21 HCSB

## THE FOCUS FOR TODAY

True contentment comes from godliness in the heart,
not from wealth in the hand.

Warren Wiersbe

A ll too often we focus our thoughts and energies on the accumulation of earthly treasures, creating untold stress in our lives and leaving precious little time to accumulate the only treasures that really matter: the spiritual kind. Our material possessions have the potential to do great good—depending upon how we use them. If we allow the things we own to own us, we may pay dearly for our misplaced priorities.

Society focuses intently on material possessions, but God's Word teaches us time and again that money matters little when compared to the spiritual gifts that the Creator offers to those who put Him first in their lives. So today, keep your possessions in perspective. Remember that God should come first, and everything else next. When you give God His rightful place in your heart, you'll have a clearer vision of the things that really matter. Then, you can joyfully thank your Heavenly Father for spiritual blessings that are, in truth, too numerous to count.

## OUR REAL RICHES

How important are your material possessions? Not as important as you might think. In the life of a committed Christian, material possessions should play a rather small role. In fact, when we become overly enamored with the things we own, we needlessly distance ourselves from the peace that God offers to those who place Him at the center of their lives.

Of course, we all need the basic necessities of life, but once we meet those needs for ourselves and for our families, the piling up of possessions creates more problems than it solves. Our real riches, of course, are not of this world. We are never really rich until we are rich in spirit.

Do you find yourself wrapped up in the concerns of the material world? If so, it's time to reorder your priorities by turning your thoughts and your prayers to more important matters. And, it's time to begin storing up riches that will endure throughout eternity: the spiritual kind.

---

### SOMETHING TO REMEMBER

The world wants you to believe that money and possessions can buy happiness. Don't believe it! Genuine happiness comes not from money, but from the things that money can't buy—starting, of course, with your relationship to God and His only begotten Son.

## MORE FROM GOD'S WORD ABOUT MATERIALISM

*Do not love the world or the things in the world. If anyone loves the world, the love of the Father is not in him.*

1 John 2:15 NKJV

*He who trusts in his riches will fall, but the righteous will flourish . . . .*

Proverbs 11:28 NKJV

*For what will it profit a man if he gains the whole world, and loses his own soul? Or what will a man give in exchange for his soul?*

Mark 8:36-37 NKJV

*For where your treasure is, there your heart will be also.*

Luke 12:34 NKJV

*Since we entered the world penniless and will leave it penniless, if we have bread on the table and shoes on our feet, that's enough.*

1 Timothy 6:7-8 MSG

## MORE POWERFUL IDEAS ABOUT MATERIALISM

The socially prescribed affluent, middle-class lifestyle has become so normative in our churches that we discern little conflict between it and the Christian lifestyle prescribed in the New Testament.

Tony Campolo

A society that pursues pleasure runs the risk of raising expectations ever higher, so that true contentment always lies tantalizingly out of reach.

Philip Yancey and Paul Brand

Greed is enslaving. The more you have, the more you want—until eventually avarice consumes you.

Kay Arthur

Here's a simple test: If you can see it, it's not going to last. The things that last are the things you cannot see.

Dennis Swanberg

The cross is laid on every Christian. It begins with the call to abandon the attachments of this world.

Dietrich Bonhoeffer

## QUESTIONS TO CONSIDER

Do I genuinely understand that material possessions will not bring me lasting happiness? Do I understand that my possessions are actually God's possessions, and do I use those possessions for His purposes?

_____

_____

Do my spending habits reflect the values that I hold most dear, and am I a faithful steward of my resources?

_____

_____

## A PRAYER FOR TODAY

*Heavenly Father, when I focus intently upon You,
I am blessed. When I focus too intently on material
possessions, I am troubled. Make my priorities pleasing
to You, Father, and make me a worthy
servant of Your Son. Amen*

## Day 25

# FINDING STRENGTH

*I can do all things through Christ who strengthens me.*
Philippians 4:13 NKJV

## THE FOCUS FOR TODAY

When trials come your way—as inevitably they will—
do not run away. Run to your God and Father.
Kay Arthur

God's love and support never changes. From the cradle to the grave, God has promised to give you the strength to meet any challenge. God has promised to lift you up and guide your steps if you let Him. God has promised that when you entrust your life to Him completely and without reservation, He will give you the courage to face any trial and the wisdom to live in His righteousness.

God's hand uplifts those who turn their hearts and prayers to Him. Will you count yourself among that number? Will you accept God's peace and wear God's armor against the temptations and distractions of our dangerous world? If you do, you can live courageously and optimistically, knowing that you have been forever touched by the loving, unfailing, uplifting hand of God.

## HE IS SUFFICIENT

Of this you can be certain: God is sufficient to meet your needs. Period.

Do the demands of life seem overwhelming at times? If so, you must learn to rely not only upon your own resources, but also upon the promises of your Father in heaven. God will hold your hand and walk with you and your family if you let Him. So even if your circumstances are difficult, trust the Father.

God promises that He is "near to those who have a broken heart" (Psalm 34:18 NKJV). When we are troubled, we must turn to Him, and we must encourage our friends and family members to do likewise.

If you are discouraged by the inevitable demands of life here on earth, be mindful of this fact: the loving heart of God is sufficient to meet any challenge . . . including yours.

---

### SOMETHING TO REMEMBER

The next time you're tempted to give up on yourself, remember that God will never, never, never give up on you. And with God in your corner, you have nothing to fear.

## MORE FROM GOD'S WORD ABOUT FINDING STRENGTH

*Be strong! We must prove ourselves strong for our people and for the cities of our God. May the Lord's will be done.*

1 Chronicles 19:13 HCSB

*And He said to me, "My grace is sufficient for you, for My strength is made perfect in weakness."*

2 Corinthians 12:9 NKJV

*Finally, be strengthened by the Lord and by His vast strength.*

Ephesians 6:10 HCSB

*The LORD is my strength and my song . . . .*

Exodus 15:2 NIV

*Those who hope in the LORD will renew their strength. They will soar on wings like eagles; they will run and not grow weary, they will walk and not be faint.*

Isaiah 40:31 NIV

## MORE POWERFUL IDEAS ABOUT FINDING STRENGTH

The same God who empowered Samson, Gideon, and Paul seeks to empower my life and your life, because God hasn't changed.

Bill Hybels

A divine strength is given to those who yield themselves to the Father and obey what He tells them to do.

Warren Wiersbe

If we take God's program, we can have God's power—not otherwise.

E. Stanley Jones

No matter how heavy the burden, daily strength is given, so I expect we need not give ourselves any concern as to what the outcome will be. We must simply go forward.

Annie Armstrong

All the power of God—the same power that hung the stars in place and put the planets in their courses and transformed Earth—now resides in you to energize and strengthen you to become the person God created you to be.

Anne Graham Lotz

## QUESTIONS TO CONSIDER

Do I gain strength and courage when I allow Christ to dwell in the center of my heart?

_____

_____

Do I gain strength through prayer?

_____

_____

Do I understand the importance of regular exercise and sensible rest?

_____

_____

### A PRAYER FOR TODAY

*Lord, sometimes life is difficult. Sometimes, I am worried, weary, or heartbroken. But, when I lift my eyes to You, Father, You strengthen me. When I am weak, You lift me up. Today, I turn to You, Lord, for my strength, for my hope, and my salvation. Amen*

# Day 26

# THE NEED TO FORGIVE

*Get rid of all bitterness, rage, anger, harsh words,*
*and slander, as well as all types of malicious behavior.*
*Instead, be kind to each other, tenderhearted, forgiving one*
*another, just as God through Christ has forgiven you.*

Ephesians 4:31-32 NLT

## THE FOCUS FOR TODAY

To be a Christian means to forgive the inexcusable,
because God has forgiven the inexcusable in you.

C. S. Lewis

I t has been said that life is an exercise in forgiveness. And it should be added that forgiveness is an essential step in overcoming tough times.

Christ understood the importance of forgiveness when He commanded, "Love your enemies and pray for those who persecute you" (Matthew 5:43-44 NIV). But sometimes, forgiveness is difficult indeed.

When we have been injured or embarrassed, we feel the urge to strike back and to hurt the ones who have hurt us. But Christ instructs us to do otherwise. Christ teaches us that forgiveness is God's way and that mercy is an integral part of God's plan for our lives. In short, we are commanded to weave the thread of forgiveness into the very fabric of our lives.

Do you invest more time than you should reliving the past? Are you troubled by feelings of anger, bitterness, envy, or regret? Do you harbor ill will against someone whom you simply can't seem to forgive? If so, it's time to finally get serious about forgiveness.

When someone hurts you, the act of forgiveness is difficult, but necessary. Until you forgive, you are trapped in a prison of your own creation. But what if you have tried to forgive and simply can't seem to do so? The solution to your dilemma is this: you simply must make forgiveness a higher priority in your life.

Most of us don't spend too much time thinking about forgiveness; we worry, instead, about the injustices we have suffered and the people who inflicted them. God has a better plan: He wants us to live in the present, not the past, and He knows that in order to do so, we must forgive those who have harmed us.

Have you made forgiveness a high priority? Have you sincerely asked God to forgive you for your inability to forgive others? Have you genuinely prayed that those feelings of anger might be swept from your heart? If so, congratulations. If not, perhaps it's time to move past your own particular tough times by freeing yourself from the chains of bitterness and regret.

SOMETHING TO REMEMBER

Today, think about the people you still need to forgive. And then ask God to help you forgive them. Remember that when you forgive other people, you're giving yourself a gift. And, remember that God doesn't say that forgiveness is optional; it's a commandment.

## MORE FROM GOD'S WORD ABOUT
## THE NEED TO FORGIVE

*And whenever you stand praying, if you have anything against anyone, forgive him, so that your Father in heaven may also forgive you your wrongdoing.*

Mark 11:25 HCSB

*For if you forgive people their wrongdoing, your heavenly Father will forgive you as well. But if you don't forgive people, your Father will not forgive your wrongdoing.*

Matthew 6:14-15 HCSB

*Blessed are the merciful, because they will be shown mercy.*

Matthew 5:7 HCSB

*You have heard that it was said, You shall love your neighbor and hate your enemy. But I tell you, love your enemies, and pray for those who persecute you, so that you may be sons of your Father in heaven.*

Matthew 5:43-45 HCSB

*Then Peter came to Him and said, "Lord, how many times could my brother sin against me and I forgive him? As many as seven times?" "I tell you, not as many as seven," Jesus said to him, "but 70 times seven."*

Matthew 18:21-22 HCSB

## MORE POWERFUL IDEAS ABOUT
## THE NEED TO FORGIVE

God expects us to forgive others as He has forgiven us; we are to follow His example by having a forgiving heart.

*Vonette Bright*

How often should you forgive the other person? Only as many times as you want God to forgive you!

*Marie T. Freeman*

Forgiveness is actually the best revenge because it not only sets us free from the person we forgive, but it frees us to move into all that God has in store for us.

*Stormie Omartian*

I believe that forgiveness can become a continuing cycle: because God forgives us, we're to forgive others; because we forgive others, God forgives us. Scripture presents both parts of the cycle.

*Shirley Dobson*

Forgiveness is the key that unlocks the door of resentment and the handcuffs of hate. It is a power that breaks the chains of bitterness and the shackles of selfishness.

*Corrie ten Boom*

## QUESTIONS TO CONSIDER

Am I willing to acknowledge the important role that forgiveness should play in my life?

_____

_____

Will I strive to forgive those who have hurt me, even when doing so is difficult?

_____

_____

Do I understand that forgiveness is a marathon (not a sprint), and will I prayerfully ask God to help me move beyond the emotions of bitterness and regret?

_____

_____

### A PRAYER FOR TODAY

_Heavenly Father, forgiveness is Your commandment, and I know that I should forgive others just as You have forgiven me. But, genuine forgiveness is difficult. Help me to forgive those who have injured me, and deliver me from the traps of anger and bitterness. Forgiveness is Your way, Lord; let it be mine. Amen_

# Day 27

# TIME TO GET BUSY

*And whatever you do, do it heartily, as to the Lord
and not to men.*
Colossians 3:23 NKJV

## THE FOCUS FOR TODAY

Let us not be content to wait and see what will happen,
but give us the determination
to make the right things happen.
Peter Marshall

I t isn't easy to overcome tough times—it takes hard work and lots of it. So if you're facing adversity of any kind, you can be sure that God has important work for you to do . . . but He won't make you do it. Since the days of Adam and Eve, God has allowed His children to make choices for themselves, and so it is with you. You can either dig in and work hard, or you can retreat to the couch, click on the TV, and hope things get better on their own.

The Bible instructs us that we can learn an important lesson of a surprising source: ants. Ants are among nature's most industrious creatures. They do their work without supervision, rumination, or hesitation. We should do likewise. When times are tough, we must summon the courage and determination to work ourselves out of trouble.

God has created a world in which diligence is rewarded and sloth is not. So whatever you choose to do, do it with commitment, excitement, and vigor. God didn't create you for a life of mediocrity or pain; He created you for far greater things. Reaching for greater things—and defeating tough times—usually requires work and lots of it, which is perfectly fine with God. After all, He knows that you're up to the task, and He still has big plans for you. Very big plans . . .

## WHEREVER YOU ARE, WORK HARD

Wherever you find yourself, whatever your job description, do your work, and do it with all your heart. When you do, you will most certainly win the recognition of your peers. But more importantly, God will bless your efforts and use you in ways that only He can understand. So do your work with focus and dedication. And leave the rest up to God.

---

### SOMETHING TO REMEMBER

Today, pick out one important obligation that you've been putting off. Then, take at least one specific step toward the completion of the task you've been avoiding. Even if you don't finish the job, you'll discover that it's easier to finish a job that you've already begun than to finish a job that you've never started.

## MORE FROM GOD'S WORD ABOUT
## THE NEED TO TAKE ACTION

*For the Kingdom of God is not just fancy talk; it is living by God's power.*

1 Corinthians 4:20 NLT

*Therefore, get your minds ready for action, being self-disciplined, and set your hope completely on the grace to be brought to you at the revelation of Jesus Christ.*

1 Peter 1:13 HCSB

*But prove yourselves doers of the word, and not merely hearers.*

James 1:22 NASB

*Are there those among you who are truly wise and understanding? Then they should show it by living right and doing good things with a gentleness that comes from wisdom.*

James 3:13 NCV

*The prudent see danger and take refuge, but the simple keep going and suffer from it.*

Proverbs 27:12 NIV

## MORE POWERFUL IDEAS ABOUT
## THE NEED TO TAKE ACTION

Action springs not from thought, but from a readiness for responsibility.

*Dietrich Bonhoeffer*

God has lots of folks who intend to go to work for him "some day." What He needs is more people who are willing to work for Him this day.

*Marie T. Freeman*

Paul did one thing. Most of us dabble in forty things. Are you a doer or a dabbler?

*Vance Havner*

Logic will not change an emotion, but action will.

*Zig Ziglar*

It is by acts and not by ideas that people live.

*Harry Emerson Fosdick*

Pray as if it's all up to God, and work as if it's all up to you.

*Anonymous*

## QUESTIONS TO CONSIDER

When I have work that needs to be done, do I usually try to finish the work as soon as possible, or do I put it off?

_____

_____

Do I believe that my testimony is more powerful when actions accompany my words?

_____

_____

Do I see the hypocrisy in saying one thing and doing another, and do I try my best to act in accordance with my beliefs?

_____

_____

### A PRAYER FOR TODAY

*Heavenly Father, when I am fearful, keep me mindful that You are my protector and my salvation. Give me strength, Lord, to face the challenges of this day as I gain my courage from You. Amen*

# Day 28

# TIME FOR RENEWAL

*I will give you a new heart and put a new spirit within you.*
Ezekiel 36:26 HCSB

## THE FOCUS FOR TODAY

God specializes in things fresh and firsthand.
His plans for you this year may outshine those of the past.
He's prepared to fill your days with reasons
to give Him praise.

Joni Eareckson Tada

On occasion, the demands of daily life can drain us of our strength and rob us of the joy that is rightfully ours in Christ. When we find ourselves tired, discouraged, or worse, there is a source from which we can draw the power needed to recharge our spiritual batteries. That source is God.

Is your spiritual battery running low? Is your energy on the wane? Are your emotions frayed? If so, it's time to turn your thoughts and your prayers to your Heavenly Father. When you do, He will provide for your needs, and He will restore your soul.

## UNDERSTANDING DEPRESSION

Throughout our lives, all of us must endure personal losses that leave us struggling to find hope. The sadness that accompanies such losses is an inescapable fact of life—but in time, we move beyond our grief as the sadness runs its course and life returns to normal. Depression, however, is more than sadness . . . much more.

Depression is a physical and emotional condition that is, in almost all cases, treatable with medication and counseling. And it is not a disease to be taken lightly. Left untreated, depression presents real dangers to patients' physical health and to their emotional well-being.

If you're feeling blue, perhaps it's a logical response to the disappointments of everyday life. But if your feelings of sadness have lasted longer than you think they should— or if someone close to you fears that your sadness may have evolved into clinical depression—it's time to seek professional help.

Here are a few simple guidelines to consider as you make decisions about possible medical treatment:

1. If your feelings of sadness have resulted in persistent and prolonged changes in sleep patterns, or if you've experienced a significant change in weight (either gain or loss), consult your physician. 2. If you have persistent urges toward self-destructive behavior, or if you feel as though you have lost the will to live, consult a professional counselor or physician immediately. 3. If someone you trust urges you to seek counseling, schedule a session with a professionally trained counselor to evaluate your condition. 4. If you are plagued by consistent, prolonged, severe feelings of hopelessness, consult a physician, a professional counselor, or your pastor.

God's Word has much to say about every aspect of your life, including your emotional health. And, when you face concerns of any sort—including symptoms of depression—remember that God is with you. Your Creator intends that His joy should become your joy. Yet sometimes, amid the inevitable hustle and bustle of life-here-on-earth, you may forfeit—albeit temporarily—God's joy as you wrestle with the challenges of daily living.

So, if you're feeling genuinely depressed, trust your medical doctor to do his or her part. Then, place your ultimate trust in your benevolent Heavenly Father. His healing touch, like His love, endures forever.

### SOMETHING TO REMEMBER

God wants to give you peace, and He wants to renew your spirit. It's up to you to slow down and give Him a chance to do so.

## MORE FROM GOD'S WORD ABOUT RENEWAL

*The One who was sitting on the throne said, "Look! I am making everything new!" Then he said, "Write this, because these words are true and can be trusted."*

Revelation 21:5 NCV

*When doubts filled my mind, your comfort gave me renewed hope and cheer.*

Psalm 94:19 NLT

*Create in me a pure heart, O God, and renew a steadfast spirit within me. Do not cast me from your presence or take your Holy Spirit from me. Restore to me the joy of your salvation and grant me a willing spirit, to sustain me.*

Psalm 51:10-12 NIV

*He makes me to lie down in green pastures; He leads me beside the still waters. He restores my soul; He leads me in the paths of righteousness for His name's sake.*

Psalm 23:2–3 NKJV

*Come to Me, all you who labor and are heavy laden, and I will give you rest. Take My yoke upon you and learn from Me, for I am gentle and lowly in heart, and you will find rest for your souls. For My yoke is easy and My burden is light.*

Matthew 11:28-30 NKJV

## MORE POWERFUL IDEAS ABOUT RENEWAL

He is the God of wholeness and restoration.

Stormie Omartian

Repentance removes old sins and wrong attitudes, and it opens the way for the Holy Spirit to restore our spiritual health.

Shirley Dobson

God gives us permission to forget our past and the understanding to live our present. He said He will remember our sins no more. (Psalm 103:11-12)

Serita Ann Jakes

Each of us has something broken in our lives: a broken promise, a broken dream, a broken marriage, a broken heart . . . and we must decide how we're going to deal with our brokenness. We can wallow in self-pity or regret, accomplishing nothing and having no fun or joy in our circumstances; or we can determine with our will to take a few risks, get out of our comfort zone, and see what God will do to bring unexpected delight in our time of need.

Luci Swindoll

Walking with God leads to
receiving his intimate counsel,
and counseling leads
to deep restoration.

—

John Eldredge

## QUESTIONS TO CONSIDER

Do I believe that God can make all things new—including me?

_____

_____

Do I take time each day to be still and let God give me perspective and direction?

_____

_____

Do I understand the importance of getting a good night's sleep?

_____

_____

## A PRAYER FOR TODAY

_Lord, You are my rock and my strength. When I grow weary, let me turn my thoughts and my prayers to You. When I am discouraged, restore my faith in You. Let me always trust in Your promises, Lord, and let me draw strength from those promises and from Your unending love. Amen_

# Day 29

# A RENEWED SENSE OF PURPOSE

*You will show me the way of life, granting me the joy of your presence and the pleasures of living with you forever.*

Psalm 16:11 NLT

## THE FOCUS FOR TODAY

God will make obstacles serve His purpose.

Mrs. Charles E. Cowman

I f you're experiencing tough times, you may be asking yourself "What does God want me to do next?" Perhaps you're pondering your future, uncertain of your plans, unsure of your next step. But even if you don't have a clear plan for the next step of your life's journey, you may rest assured that God does.

God has a plan for the universe, and He has a plan for you. He understands that plan as thoroughly and completely as He knows you. If you seek God's will earnestly and prayerfully, He will make His plans known to you in His own time and in His own way.

Do you sincerely want to discover God's purpose for your life? If so, you must first be willing to live in accordance with His commandments. You must also study God's Word and be watchful for His signs. Finally, you should open yourself up to the Creator every day—beginning with this one—and you must have faith that He will soon reveal His plans to you.

Perhaps your vision of God's purpose for your life has been clouded by a wish list that you have expected God to dutifully fulfill. Perhaps, you have fervently hoped that God would create a world that unfolds according to your wishes, not His. If so, you have probably experienced more disappointment than satisfaction and more frustration than peace. A better strategy is to conform your will to

God's (and not to struggle vainly in an attempt to conform His will to yours).

Sometimes, God's plans and purposes may seem unmistakably clear to you. If so, push ahead. But other times, He may lead you through the wilderness before He directs you to the Promised Land. So be patient and keep seeking His will for your life. When you do, you'll be amazed at the marvelous things that an all-powerful, all-knowing God can do.

---

### SOMETHING TO REMEMBER

Perhaps you're in a hurry to understand God's unfolding plan for your life. If so, remember that God operates according to a perfect timetable. That timetable is His, not yours. So be patient. God may have quite a few lessons to teach you before you are fully prepared to do His will and fulfill His purpose.

---

## MORE FROM GOD'S WORD ABOUT PURPOSE

*Whatever you do, do all to the glory of God.*

1 Corinthians 10:31 NKJV

*You're sons of Light, daughters of Day. We live under wide open skies and know where we stand. So let's not sleepwalk through life . . . .*

1 Thessalonians 5:5-6 MSG

*We look at this Son and see the God who cannot be seen. We look at this Son and see God's original purpose in everything created.*

Colossians 1:15 MSG

*To everything there is a season, a time for every purpose under heaven.*

Ecclesiastes 3:1 NKJV

*There is one thing I always do. Forgetting the past and straining toward what is ahead, I keep trying to reach the goal and get the prize for which God called me . . . .*

Philippians 3:13–14 NCV

## More Powerful Ideas About Purpose

Underneath each trouble there is a faithful purpose.

C. H. Spurgeon

God does not discipline us to subdue us, but to condition us for a life of usefulness and blessedness.

Billy Graham

Some virtues cannot be produced in us without affliction.

C. H. Spurgeon

When the sovereign God brings us to nothing, it is to reroute our lives, not to end them.

Charles Swindoll

We should not be upset when unexpected and upsetting things happen. God, in His wisdom, means to make something of us which we have not yet attained, and He is dealing with us accordingly.

J. I. Packer

Whatever clouds you face today, ask Jesus, the light of the world, to help you look behind the cloud to see His glory and His plans for you.

Billy Graham

## QUESTIONS TO CONSIDER

Do I understand the importance of discovering (or rediscovering, if necessary) God's unfolding purpose for my life?

_____

_____

Do I consult God on matters great and small?

_____

_____

Do I pray about my plans for the future, and do I remain open to the opportunities and challenges that God places before me.

_____

_____

## A PRAYER FOR TODAY

*Dear Lord, let Your purposes be my purposes. Let Your priorities be my priorities. Let Your will be my will. Let Your Word be my guide. And, let me grow in faith and in wisdom today and every day. Amen*

# Day 30

# FOLLOW HIM

*Then Jesus said to His disciples, "If anyone wants to come with Me, he must deny himself, take up his cross, and follow Me. For whoever wants to save his life will lose it, but whoever loses his life because of Me will find it."*

Matthew 16:24-25 HCSB

## THE FOCUS FOR TODAY

You who suffer take heart.
Christ is the answer to sorrow.

Billy Graham

J esus walks with you. Are you walking with Him seven days a week, and not just on Sunday mornings? Are you a seven-day-a-week Christian who carries your faith with you to work each day, or do you try to keep Jesus at a "safe" distance when you're not sitting in church? Hopefully, you understand the wisdom of walking with Christ all day every day.

Jesus loved you so much that He endured unspeakable humiliation and suffering for you. How will you respond to Christ's sacrifice? Will you take up His cross and follow Him—during good times and tough times—or will you choose another path? When you place your hopes squarely at the foot of the cross, when you place Jesus squarely at the center of your life, you will be blessed.

Do you seek to fulfill God's purpose for your life? Do you seek spiritual abundance? Would you like to partake in "the peace that passes all understanding"? Then follow Christ. Follow Him by picking up His cross today and every day that you live. When you do, you will quickly discover that Christ's love has the power to change everything, including you.

## YOUR ETERNAL JOURNEY

Eternal life is not an event that begins when you die. Eternal life begins when you invite Jesus into your heart right here on earth. So it's important to remember that God's plans for you are not limited to the ups and downs of everyday life. If you've allowed Jesus to reign over your heart, you've already begun your eternal journey.

Today, give praise to the Creator for His priceless gift, the gift of eternal life. And then, when you've offered Him your thanks and your praise, share His Good News with all who cross your path.

---

### SOMETHING TO REMEMBER

Following Christ is a matter of obedience. If you want to be a little more like Jesus . . . learn about His teachings, follow in His footsteps, and obey His commandments.

---

## MORE FROM GOD'S WORD ABOUT
## FOLLOWING CHRIST

*Then he told them what they could expect for themselves: "Anyone who intends to come with me has to let me lead."*

Luke 9:23 MSG

*I've laid down a pattern for you. What I've done, you do.*

John 13:15 MSG

*No one can serve two masters. Either he will hate the one and love the other, or he will be devoted to the one and despise the other.*

Matthew 6:24 NIV

*Whoever is not willing to carry the cross and follow me is not worthy of me. Those who try to hold on to their lives will give up true life. Those who give up their lives for me will hold on to true life.*

Matthew 10:38-39 NCV

*If anyone would come after me, he must deny himself and take up his cross and follow me.*

Mark 8:34 NIV

## More Powerful Ideas About Following Christ

Jesus Christ is not a security from storms. He is perfect security in storms.

Kathy Troccoli

In the midst of the pressure and the heat, I am confident His hand is on my life, developing my faith until I display His glory, transforming me into a vessel of honor that pleases Him!

Anne Graham Lotz

Sometimes we get tired of the burdens of life, but we know that Jesus Christ will meet us at the end of life's journey. And, that makes all the difference.

Billy Graham

The Lord gets His best soldiers out of the highlands of affliction.

C. H. Spurgeon

God takes us through struggles and difficulties so that we might become increasingly committed to Him.

Charles Swindoll

## QUESTIONS TO CONSIDER

Do I really believe that my relationship with Jesus should be one of servant and Master? And am I behaving like His servant?

_____

_____

Am I attempting to follow in Christ's footsteps, despite my imperfections?

_____

_____

Do I sense a joyful abundance that is mine when I follow Christ?

_____

_____

### A PRAYER FOR TODAY

_Dear Jesus, because I am Your disciple, I will trust You, I will obey Your teachings, and I will share Your Good News. You have given me life abundant and life eternal, and I will follow You today and forever. Amen_